LUCY CALKINS AND PAT BLEICHMAN

The Craft of Revision

DEDICATION

To Kathleen Tolan, whose brilliant and passionate professional development has changed the face of New York City schools.

*first*hand

FirstHand
An imprint of Heinemann
A division of Reed Elsevier Inc.
361 Hanover Street
Portsmouth, NH 03801-3912
www.heinemann.com

Offices and agents throughout the world

Photography: Peter Cunningham

The author and publisher wish to thank those who have generously given permission to reprint borrowed material:

Excerpts from *Owl Moon* by Jane Yolen. Text Copyright © 1987 by Jane Yolen. Used by permission of Philomel Books, a division of Penguin Young Readers Group, a member of Penguin Group (USA) Inc., New York, NY. All rights reserved.

Excerpts from *The Relatives Came* by Cynthia Rylant. Text Copyright © 1985 by Cynthia Rylant. Reprinted with the permission of Simon & Schuster Books for Young Readers, an imprint of Simon & Schuster Children's Publishing Division.

Rubrics and checklists adapted by permission from *New Standards*. The *New Standards*® assessment system includes performance standards with performance descriptions, student work samples and commentaries, on-demand examinations, and a portfolio system. For more information, contact the National Center on Education and the Economy, 202-783-3668 or www.ncee.org.

Library of Congress Cataloging-in-Publication Data
Calkins, Lucy McCormick.
    The craft of revision / Lucy Calkins and Pat Bleichman.
        p. cm. — (Units of study for primary writing ; 4)
    ISBN 0-325-00527-3 (pbk. : alk. paper)
        1. English language-Composition and exercises-Study and teaching (Primary)--United States. 2. Editing-Study and teaching
            (Primary)—United States. 3. Curriculum planning-United States. I. Bleichman, Pat. II. Title.
    LB1529.U5C353 2003   2003019533
    372.62'3--dc22

Printed in the United States of America on acid-free paper

07   06   05   04   ML   3   4   5

SERIES COMPONENTS

▸ **The Nuts and Bolts of Teaching Writing** provides a comprehensive overview of the processes and structures of the primary writing workshop.

▸ You'll use **The Conferring Handbook** as you work with individual students to identify and address specific writing issues.

▸ The seven **Units of Study**, each covering approximately four weeks of instruction, give you the strategies, lesson plans, and tools you'll need to teach writing to your students in powerful, lasting ways. Presented sequentially, the Units take your children from oral and pictorial story telling, through emergent and into fluent writing.

▸ To support your writing program, the **Resources for Primary Writers CD-ROM** provides video and print resources. You'll find clips of the authors teaching some of the lessons, booklists, supplementary material, **reproducibles** and **overheads**.

THE CRAFT OF REVISION

Across the nation, there is growing agreement that teachers must not only assign and correct writing, but that we must also teach children the process of writing that all writers use. Revision is at the heart of that writing process. When I was a child, no one told me that there is a process that is as fundamental to writing as the scientific method is to science. But since those days, the teaching of writing has been revolutionized. Now, when a school or a district decides to teach writing as a process, this means that revision becomes a priority.

Why This Unit?

When my colleagues and I convened to plan a yearlong curriculum in the teaching of writing, we began by asking, "What matters most?" We couldn't grant unit-of-study status to all our priorities; there wasn't time enough in a school year to create month-long inquiries into qualities of good writing and partnerships, descriptive and narrative writing, how-to books and book reviews. Hard choices had to be made. None of us debated, however, whether revision was worthy of this sort of priority status. Our commitment to revision was part and parcel of our commitment to teaching writing as a process.

Writing is a powerful tool for thinking for the precise reason that when we write, we can take fleeting and intangible memories, insights, and images and make them concrete. When we talk, our thoughts float away. When we write, we put our thoughts onto paper. We can stick them in our pocket. We can come back to them later. We can show our thoughts to our friends. We can hold our ideas in our hands and think

about our thinking. "I think this idea has two parts," we muse. We reread our first thoughts and see gaps in them. We look again and see connections between two different sets of ideas. In this way, it is through rereading and revision that writing becomes a tool for thinking. When we revise, we hold our thoughts in our hands and think about our thinking.

About the Unit

The question my colleagues and I wrestled with, then, was not whether revision is fundamental to writing but whether it is within the grasp of young children. "You don't expect *kindergartners* to revise, do you?" teachers sometimes ask, their voices filled with skepticism. My colleagues and I believe that revision is well suited to kindergarten and first-grade children. Watch a child at work making something—anything—and one sees revision. The child pats a ball of clay into a pancake to make a duck pond, and then revises the duck pond by creating a fingertip rainstorm that dapples the water surface. Soon she is in the dress-up area with a shawl draped over her shoulders and a pocketbook in hand saying, "Pretend I'm the mommy." Then, lighting upon a better idea, she pulls the shawl up over her head and stoops her shoulders. "No, I'm the Granny." Young children revise block castles to add protected hiding spots for archers, and they revise pictures of spaceships to add explosions. Young children can revise their writing with equal ease and enthusiasm—as long as we don't expect their revisions to look like those a grown-up would make. First graders can revise—as long as we expect their six-year-old best!

I remember when Jolene brought me a book she'd written called *My Hamster*. The book included a few details about the furry fellow, but then deviated into being a book about Jolene's dad. "You may want to take this apart and make two books," I suggested. "One could be on your hamster; one could be on your dad. Because right now this title says *My Hamster* (I pointed to the title), but half the book is about something else!" Jolene was quiet for a moment, her eyes scanning the story. Then she said, "I know!" and jumped up. I expected her to return with scissors but instead she brought a magic marker. Beside the title "My Hamster," she added, "and My Father and School and Other Stuff."

Greg, one of Jolene's classmates, often reread his books and, with arrows, added information he'd forgotten to include. Sometimes he used Jaws, the class staple-remover, to remove the staples from his homemade books and then he would lay the pages out on his table and think, "Wait. What order should these go in?" When I arrived in Greg's first-grade classroom one morning, he paused for a moment to tell me his agenda for the writing workshop. "I'm going to revise my Hermy books," he said, "because people like them. Revise means adding some tips. If you read my book and you find a place where nothing makes sense, give me a holler and I'll revise, or I'll take out that page." Writers like Greg know that revision is not an afterthought, it is a part of every day's writing process.

Because my colleagues and I wanted to shine a curricular spotlight on revision, we decided to devote a month-long unit to a study of revision. Because the unit follows personal narrative work, children revise their Small Moment stories and learn not only revision strategies, but also qualities of effective narrative writing.

Bringing Our Own Writing to the Classroom

Pat Bleichman, first-grade teacher and co-author of this book, and I soon decided that if we wanted to teach our children to draft and revise their writing, we'd need to bring a real writer into the classroom, one who could show children how and why grown-up writers cut and tape and add and reorder . . . and that real writer would need to be us!

Pat wasn't too sure about the idea of working on her own creative writing. "You see, Lucy," she said, "when I was a kid, I was never taught to write, really. I'm not that confident as a writer." I knew just what Pat meant. When I first taught, the principal of my school played the guitar. He'd gather the school community in an assembly in which children raised the rafters with songs that made our hearts swell. "If I had a hammer, I'd hammer in the morning," they'd sing. The more I heard music filling every nook and cranny of our school, the worse I felt. It was fine and dandy for *them* to sing with their classes—*they* could sing! But my singing voice resembled that of a cow. My face blushed at the mere thought of singing publicly with my class.

My principal would hear none of my protests. "Lucy," he said, "they need you to belt out those songs. You don't need to be good at this. They won't know the difference. But they need *you*, the one they love, to sing with your full heart and voice." And so, with trepidation, I closed my classroom door, and we sang. Now, years later, when I think back on my very first years as a teacher, I can still feel the camaraderie of singing together, raising our hearts and voices as one. The funny thing is, I learned that my voice wasn't as bad as I thought after all, and ever since, I've sung as I go through my days. Pat, the other co-authors, and I agreed that one of the best things about teaching young kids is that they admire us even when our clothes aren't fashionable, our bodies svelte, or our voices in tune. They don't need us to be perfect, but they *do* need us to jump in and do whatever we're asking them to do and to be public learners.

Pat and I decided, in preparation for this unit, that we'd write and revise our own personal narratives and share what we did and learned with our students. As we worked, we maintained a double focus, paying attention both to strategies we asked children to use and to our own experiences as we tried to write and revise our own writing. We knew, in the end, that the writing we did would yield two kinds of stories—narratives of our own personal lives, and narratives of our writing lives. And we knew that both kinds of texts would enrich our teaching.

One of our "ah-ha's" came when we realized that, in the past, we'd taught children *strategies* for revision (such as the technique of using a carat to insert more into a text or the strategy of "stretching" a line by turning it into a paragraph), but that none of these activities could be regarded as a strategy unless they contained an action *and* a goal. We realized there needed to be a thin line between teaching revision strategies and teaching qualities of good writing. We didn't want to merely extol children to revise their leads or their endings. What constituted a better lead or ending? How could we equip children to write more effective leads (or better character descriptions, endings, dialogue, titles, and so forth) unless we knew a lot about qualities of good writing?

I pointed out to my group that when I'd been stymied over the opening line for my first book, *Lessons from a Child*, my writing teacher, Pulitzer prize winning writer Don Murray, hadn't *just* said, "Try three leads and choose one." He hadn't *just* taught me a revision strategy. Instead, he'd also given me a particular tip about ways to start a story. Now, thirty years later, I can still recall his advice: "If you don't know what else to talk about, the weather always works," he'd said. That advice helped me write the first sentence of my first book, *Lessons from a Child*: "Shafts of sunlight angled into the small New Hampshire classroom as I. . . ." Soon many of our children were beginning their pieces by writing about the weather.

We quickly saw that not only could very young children do this revision work with their writing, they had great enthusiasm for it. With this unit of study, we tap that enthusiasm, teaching children ways to re-see, reform, and strengthen—revise—their writing and, therefore, their thinking.

INTRODUCING REVISION

GETTING READY

- Class set of new revision folders (or newly cleaned-out old folders) containing only a duplicated copy of the last story the child published
- Class set of special revision pens that are a different color
- Short, shared story (a shared class experience or a story from a previous unit) prewritten on chart paper
- Two different-colored markers to use during the lesson (one should be the same color as the original writing on the chart paper; the other, to be used for revisions, should be a contrasting color)
- Writing surface for your chart paper (ideally an easel)
- Chart paper for creating a class chart titled "Writers Revise"
- Partnerships—during the minilesson, children should sit beside their long-term partners, perhaps in assigned spots on the rug

THIS UNIT PRESUMES THAT THE CHILDREN *have already drafted a collection of pieces, from which they will spend the next month revising their favorites. Revision, then, is presented as a complement to good writing. You'll tell children that because their work will reach readers, it's important to revise toward their sense of great writing.*

To launch this unit, ask your children if they are proud of the writing they just published in the previous unit. After they respond with a resounding "Yes!" you'll deliver this surprising message: "What writers do when we really like what we've written is we revise." Your goal for today will be to convey a clear assumption that your children, like real writers, will surely want to revise, and that you will teach them strategies for doing this.

You need to prepare yourself to present revision as an opportunity and a privilege. Act as if you couldn't imagine anyone not welcoming the chance to revise. Then find ways to seal the deal. The purple pens, described in the minilesson, are one such enticement.

In this session, you'll show children how you reread and revise a story you've written, and you'll solicit children's suggestions for how you could add more details to that story.

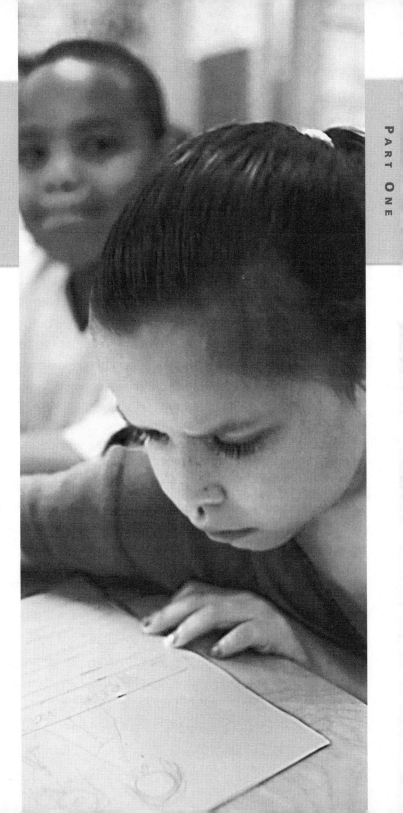

Connection

Celebrate the children's publications from the previous unit and tell children that when writers really love their writing, they revise that writing.

"Writers, I need to begin today by asking you a question. Are you all proud of the personal narratives you wrote during our last study?" Pat knew she was safe asking this question, and her children did nod vigorously and with great conviction. "Good. The reason I'm asking is that today I want to teach you what writers do when we look at our work and say, 'I like what I wrote.' When we like our writing, writers revise. We look back and we think, 'How can I make this *even better*?' From now until winter holiday, we're going to look back on the great writing we've already done, and we're going to revise that writing. And I will show you how real writers revise."

Teaching

Tell the children that today they'll revise the work they published just a few days earlier. Show them the new tools they'll use to support this work.

"I have duplicated your final publications from last time, and they are in your new revision folders, in the left, to-be-revised pocket." Pat showed them one. "You'll see that in your toolboxes, I have added cans full of purple revision pens. There are enough for all of us."

Demonstrate how you begin to revise, accentuating the techniques you want your students to use: rereading, envisioning one's subject, and asking, "How could I make this better?"

"Let me show you how to revise." Pat took hold of a purple marker, explaining as she did that their revision pens were purple too, the color of kings and queens. "First, I reread, and as I do this, I am thinking, 'This story is going to go in the library. Hundreds of people will read it. Is there *anything* I could add to make it *even better*?'" Shifting from the role of teacher to that of writer, Pat turned to a

At this point the children's heads are spinning. Can Pat mean they are going to revise the pieces that are already proudly circulating the room as finished texts? How can she be speaking with such warmth and joy about that? Pat carries on as if she is oblivious that everyone isn't 100% on board yet.

By asking children to mess up duplicated copies instead of the original drafts, Pat and I know we'll ease some of their reservations. We also know we have some wooing to do and that the special pens will go a long way! Even the new revision folders help woo children toward this work. But it is our absolute conviction that, of course, children want to revise and that makes the biggest difference.

By thinking aloud as she flips through the chart paper, Pat publicly takes on the role of writer, opening up the top of her head to let the children see the wheels of thought turning. The thoughts she has are those she hopes her children will have. She thinks aloud to emphasize that revision is purposeful and that we revise toward publication.

narrative she'd written during the previous unit. Turning the pages of her story, she muttered, "Hmm, let's see, I gotta picture this as a book in the library. "

Pat reread the story on the chart paper.

It was morning meeting.
Everyone heard a noise coming from the couch.
Patrick jumped up.
There was a mouse.

Samantha raised her hand. "I remember that. It was morning meeting, and we found the mouse in our classroom!"

"That's right, Samantha," Pat said, her eyes still on the piece, in this way signaling she didn't want a whole lot of commentary now. Pat took her purple marker. "Hmm, let's see. How can I make this story even better?"

When you revise, name the replicable strategy you use. Remind writers that they can use this strategy (in this case, adding on) often.

"I could add 'under the cushion' to the end of the piece." Pat did this with the purple revision marker. "Writers do this a lot, we add more words so readers can picture what happened."

"Okay, now let me reread it again."

It was morning meeting.
Everyone heard a noise coming from the couch.
Patrick jumped up.
There was a mouse **under the cushion.
It was tiny.**

Pat makes sure the story is very brief and simple. This isn't the time or place to dazzle children with an amazing sample of writing. Remember, your bare-bones narrative will be revised over the next few days, becoming much longer and richer. You can illustrate the benefits of revision best if the story begins as a very simple one and if it is a story that has potential to hold children's interest over time.

Pat acknowledges Samantha's comment and quickly moves on. This is not a time for retelling the event. When Pat asks, "How can I make this story even better?" she is directing this question not to the class but to herself. She is musing aloud, not soliciting them to join in a collaborative revision experience.

When you do a bit of revision, try to name the replicable strategy you have used. In this instance, Pat doesn't name what she did by saying, "I added where the mouse went," because adding "where the mouse went" is not what is replicable. That is, writers won't very often add a mouse's location to their pieces! Instead Pat says, "I added more words so readers can picture exactly what happened," which is something all writers do.

Pat makes the revisions in different-color ink so they stand out from the original text. She will use this same color to make revisions on this shared story throughout the unit.

"You see, when we revise, we take our work very seriously and we think, 'How can I make my best work even better?' I remember what happened exactly and then I reread and think, 'What could I add?'"

Active Engagement

Ask the children to join you in thinking about how you can continue to revise your story.

"Would you work with your partner and think about what else we could add to make our story even better? I'll reread it again, and then you should turn and talk to your partner about your ideas for revision."

As the partners talked about their ideas for revision, Pat listened in to what they said.

Annabelle: "She should say that Samantha jumped on the table."

Marley: "And she should tell about how we said, 'Mouse,' and she didn't believe us. She's gotta say she thought we were joking."

Jake: "Yeah. She thought it was a toy mouse."

Reconvene the class, and repeat something you heard a child say to her partner. Show children how you can revise based on the overheard suggestions. Then elicit another suggestion (or two) for revision.

"I heard lots of suggestions. Annabelle said we could add that Samantha jumped up on the table, which I think we *definitely* should do. I'll add it right here in the illustration." Pat quickly added a sketch of Samantha on the table with a speech bubble saying, "Eeek!" "Writers do that, we revise by adding details into our stories."

Pat and I know that adding on is the easiest form of revision, so this is where we choose to begin. We also know that when the children revise, most of them will add on to the ends of their pieces. Although this work doesn't look that different from any other day's writing workshop when children resume work on pieces and add to them, it didn't bother us that this first form of revision isn't anything too complicated. We deliberately want to make it easy for these children to all feel as if they are insiders in the club of people who revise. We raise the bar later, as the unit continues.

Pat is wise first to give children instructions and then to reread the text. This helps focus their talk.

If we plan to ask children to generate content for a piece of writing, it helps if the writing is about a shared experience, so that everyone is able to make a contribution.

Pat deliberately revises the illustration rather than the written text as a way to honor a form of revision that is especially accessible to her most struggling writers. She, of course, expects that throughout the unit, everyone will revise the words in their texts as well as the illustrations. Early in the unit, however, she wants to make it respectable to revise one's illustrations, so every child will feel entirely welcome in this new unit. This is a fine place to begin.

"What other ideas did you have? Jake? All eyes on Jake."

Jake: "You should say that you thought it was a toy until you went to pick it up and you screamed."

Show children how you add their suggested revisions. Name the specific tools you use (carats, inserts) to add on to your draft.

"Good idea. This is what writers do. We reread and think, 'Where should I add that? Okay, let me reread and see where it goes.'" Pat reread the story. "I'll add that right here." Pat pointed to the place in the text and used a carat to mark where to insert the additions. Then she reread the whole thing again.

> It was morning meeting.
> Everyone heard a noise coming from the couch.
> Patrick jumped up.   **We thought it was a toy mouse. And then Pat started to pick it up.**
>   **We screamed because it was a real mouse!**
> We saw there was a mouse under the cushion.^
> It was tiny.

Summarize the revision strategies you've taught and add them to a "Writers Revise" chart.

"So you all have given me great ideas for revising this writing. Let's put our strategies onto a chart."

WRITERS REVISE

* We reread and make plans.
* We reread, make a movie in our minds, and add words.
* We add details to our drawings.

Link

Ask the children to reread their published stories and to think about what they could add to improve their stories.

"So today we'll begin our new unit by doing what real writers do. In your folders, you'll each find a duplicated copy of your published piece. We need to take these stories very seriously, because they will be read by lots of people. Right now while we are on the rug, reread your stories carefully, like we reread

Pat reminds the class that Jake is speaking to all of them, not just her, and that listeners should look at the speaker.

Pat turned Jake's comment into a teaching opportunity by showing children that writers reread to locate the exact places where they'd make additions. While adding the carat, Pat could have also said to herself, "I'll use a carat and insert that information here. Writers use carats." It isn't unusual for us to mutter a bit of commentary to accompany our demonstrations.

Other children have suggestions for how to revise the mouse story, but Pat doesn't take the time to hear from more than one or two. The point of this lesson is not to add a lot to the mouse story, but to show children how to revise by rereading and adding more information.

Pat uses the chart paper entitled "Writers Revise" and quickly adds these items to it. She doesn't solicit the students' ideas as much as remind them of what she did in the demonstration by saying things like, "First we reread the piece. Remember? We should put that on the chart." This is not a quiz of lesson content, it's a summation led by Pat.

our mouse story. As you do so, think about how you could revise it. Remember what happened on the day you describe and ask, 'How could *I* revise? What could *I* add?' Get started doing that now."

After a few minutes, ask the children if they are ready to revise. Send off those who are, and keep the small group that needs more support on the rug.

"If you have an idea for how you could revise your writing, give me a thumbs-up. Okay, off you go then. You can use our new purple revision pens to do your revisions. If you're not sure how to revise, stay on the rug."

Ask members of the small group that remains on the rug to help each other think of what to revise.

"Will you two work together, and you two? Read your pieces to each other. Listeners, your job will be to listen. If anything confuses you, ask more about it. Or just say, 'Can you tell me more?' Then after the writer tells you more, say, 'You should add that!' Get started while I watch."

It is easy to get into the habit of repeating a personalized version of the minilesson to four or five children who never seem to listen to whole-group instruction. We can end up enabling dependency if we allow ourselves to spend the workshop repeating the minilesson to four or five individuals. In this instance, Pat creates a transitional structure. She keeps the kids who believe they need more help in a small group, but she offers relatively little help to the members of that group.

TIME TO CONFER

Today you'll find yourself conducting one particular kind of conference over and over. "What are you working on today?" you'll ask. Chances are, a fair number of your children will say, "I'm done." I might concur with the child. "I love that feeling, don't you?" I might say. "You get to sit back for a moment." But *then* I would continue on, saying something to the effect of, "Then, after a little rest, I do what writers across the world do. I reread and think again." It's important to demonstrate and provide guided practice so I'd soon say, "I'll show you." Soon I'll have helped the child reread his or her piece and, with prompting, tell about the aspect of the subject that will benefit from added detail. Once the child speaks well about the subject, for even just a minute, I quickly turn the oral commentary into revision suggestions. "You've got to add that! Write it right here," I say, and I may launch the child by dictating one of his or her own sentences back. See the conferences cited at right.

Be on the lookout for a child who revises well. Bring the first and revised versions of that child's work to the After-the-Workshop Share session. Also, for tomorrow's minilesson, you'll want an example of a child who wanted to add internally into his or her draft and who, therefore (with your help, presumably), stapled an extra strip of paper off the edge of his or her draft. Today, you'll probably want to conduct a conference in which a child does that work. You may deliberately do this with a child who'd benefit from being made famous.

This conference in *The Conferring Handbook* may be especially helpful today:

▶ *"This Part Is Confusing to Me"*

Also, if you have *Conferring with Primary Writers*, you may want to refer to the following conference:

▶ "As a Reader, I'd Love to Hear More About That"

Tell the whole class the story of one child who used a revision strategy.

"Writers, may I stop you? Would you bring your revision folders and come to the carpet? I want to show you the smart work Daniel did today. He got a great idea that the rest of us could try. At first he wrote this." [*Fig. I-1*]

"Then Daniel thought he could add even more to his story so he added these details." [*Fig. I-2*]

"What revisions! Would each of you show your partner the revisions *you* made today? The revised sections should be in purple. Read the pieces without the purple parts . . . then with them."

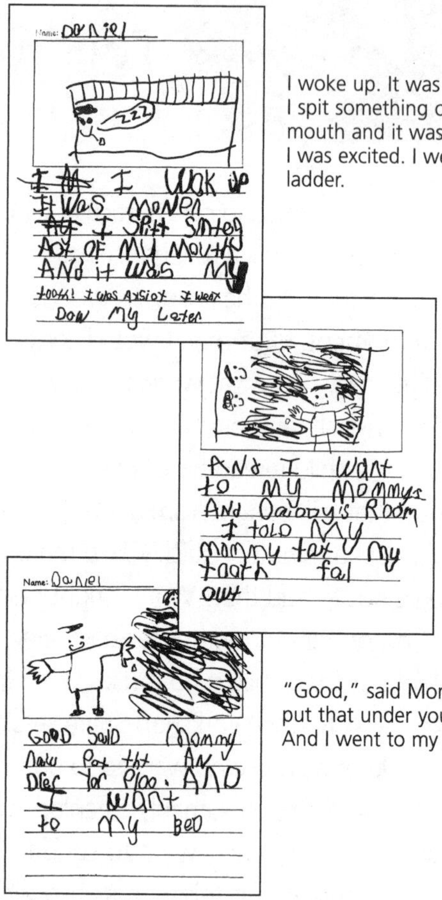

I woke up. It was morning. I spit something out of my mouth and it was my tooth! I was excited. I went down my ladder.

And I went to my mommy's and daddy's room. I told my mommy that my tooth fell out.

"Good," said Mommy. "Now put that under your pillow." And I went to my bed.

Fig. I-1   Daniel

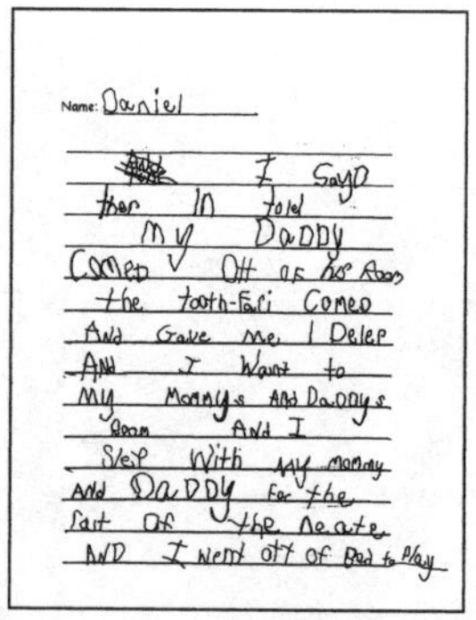

I stayed there until my daddy came out of his room. The tooth fairy came and gave me one dollar and I went to my mommy's and daddy's room. And I slept with my mommy and daddy for the rest of the night and I went out of bed to play.

Fig I-2   Daniel

IF CHILDREN NEED MORE TIME

Don't be surprised if some students need more time. You've just begun the unit. Expect that children will merely add on and call that revision, and that a fair percentage of their revisions will make their writing worse, not better. They need the opportunity to role-play their way into being the writers you hope they'll become.

You could look again at a familiar book and imagine with your class the revisions the author may have done with his or her text. For example, you might use *A Chair for My Mother* and say, "I bet when Vera Williams first wrote this book she just said she had a chair and then she probably reread what she'd written and remembered more. Then she probably said, 'Wait a minute, I could tell a lot more details.' So she probably reread her first draft and used revision paper to add details, such as. . . ."

Even if your children aren't revising much or well, move on to Sessions II and III, because these sessions address the most predictable issues that are sure to arise.

If you have supplied your children with revision pens that write in some beautiful new color, the revisions children make will stand out. Plan to glance over the work and to notice what they do in the name of revision. Ask the following questions.

- Do I see evidence that every child revised today?
- What percentage of the revisions involved adding on to the ends of texts?
- How many children revised without one-to-one prompting from me?

On this occasion, remember that you are teaching the writer, not the writing. If your writers independently initiate a process of rereading and revising, this represents progress, regardless of whether the resulting products have improved. Tell yourself, as Byrd Baylor says, that you are the one who is "in charge of celebration." If you work at it, you should be able to find reasons to celebrate. Have your writers reread? Used a carat? Added new paper? Assessed their own work? If they've done any of this, they are on a path that deserves your support. Remember how hard it is for any of us to return to and to revise work we've completed.

ADDING INTO THE MIDDLES OF TEXTS

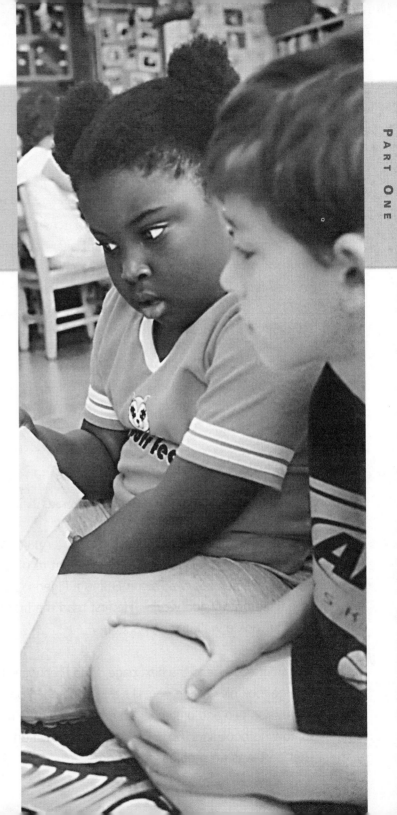

GETTING READY

▶ Sample of writing in which a child has revised first by squeezing in a line or two of writing and later by using a flap for additional space

▶ "Toolboxes" containing revision pens, scissors, staplers, and tape

▶ Paper for revisions (kindergartners may need precut strips of two-inch wide "revision paper" to tape to their pieces)

▶ Revision folders

◉ See CD-ROM for resources

IN THIS SESSION, YOU'LL GIVE CHILDREN TOOLS—*flaps for added text, carats, arrows, new pages—to make drafts malleable. They'll learn to insert new material into the middle of their drafts, not just at the end. In the previous session, in the name of revision, many children just added to the ending. If the added material actually belonged earlier in a text, these revisions often resulted in chaotically sequenced narratives. Today's session focuses on helping your children find the right place to insert new material, which will remedy some of the problems you noticed last time.*

Although today's minilesson is a step in the right direction, some texts will continue to get worse, not better. Remember, your job right now is to recruit children's enthusiastic participation in revision, so don't feel frustrated when their revisions make their pieces less focused. Celebrate the fact that they revise.

In this session, you will equip children with tools and techniques for inserting material into the middle of their drafts, and you'll teach them to reread asking, "Where should I add that?"

THE MINILESSON

Connection

Tell the children that writers use tools to revise, and today you'll introduce some.

"I've had some workmen in my kitchen lately, redoing it. And the workmen each wear those carpenter belts; have you ever seen them, belts that hold their tools? Well, yesterday while I watched you revise, I realized that someone should invent *writers'* tool belts, because we writers need a lot of tools, too. Today I am going to teach you about tools writers use when we revise. I'll show you why we need those tools."

Teaching

Tell the class about a child who reread, envisioned his content, and then revised by adding on to the end of his draft.

"I want to tell you first about a writer named George. Let me show you what George did, because you all will want to do a similar thing. First he reread his story, 'When I Saw a Falcon Eating a Pigeon.'" I held up George's book and reenacted his revision work. "He first read the first page [*Fig. II-1*], 'Once me and my dad took a walk to the park.'"

"Then he read the next page, 'And then we sat on the soccer field.' Here, George took his revision pen, like this, and added on to the end of the page." I used my revision pen and pretended to do this. "George has added the words 'to relax,' so now his book says [*Fig. II-2*], 'And then we sat on the soccer field *to relax.*' That part was no problem for George."

In this minilesson, I convey the message that revision is important by giving writers the tools of their trade. With young children, the medium is the message. If we want a child to write longer pieces, we give that child a booklet instead of a single page. If we want a child to confer with his or her partner, we create a place for doing so.

Fig. II-1   George

Once me and my dad took a walk to the park.

Fig. II-2   George

And then we sat on the soccer field *to relax.*

Until this point, I have succinctly summarized and shown the revision work George did that reflects the previous day's minilesson. This will provide a context for the new teaching I am preparing to introduce. As I turn to the teaching point, my voice becomes more serious.

Tell the class how this same child wanted to add writing where there wasn't space. Show that the child created a flap for the added writing.

"Look what happened next. George reread this page [*Fig. II-3*], 'Then we saw a falcon soaring in the air.' And he got a great idea for what he could add, but when he took up his pen to add more, he realized he *had no more room*! He came to me saying, 'I can't add anything to this page. It's already full.'"

"So let me show you what George did. He got a new sheet of paper and a *writing tool*, *these scissors*, and he did this." I modeled what George did by holding up the scissors and cutting a strip of paper.

I held up George's story. "Look!" I opened up the flap he had added and read it aloud. "'Look! It's a beautiful bird.' My dad said, 'I agree.'" [*Fig. II-3*]

"Later in the narrative, the falcon swooped down and ate the pigeon, and George again didn't have space for the words he wanted to add ('Gulp, gulp, gulp'), and again he used scissors to cut himself an extra flap of paper. Let me show you."

Besides thinking aloud during lessons, I show the actions of revision. I want the children to picture exactly what George did, and what they can do also. If this is a kindergarten class, show a child using the premade revision strips described previously. Scissoring can be a hurdle for five-year-olds, but a wonderful challenge for six-year-olds. I don't actually use the strip of paper I make; having made the strip and (I hope) my point, I now open George's draft up in such a way to show that George has already affixed such a flap onto his draft.

Then we saw a falcon soaring in the air.

"Look!" I said. "It's a beautiful bird." My dad said, "I agree."

Fig. II-3   George

Allow revision to feel like carpentry. Children will be drawn to revision if it is a physical and concrete process. The scissors, staples, and revision strips will help. Eventually, children will internalize this external, concrete work and use arrows and codes to accomplish the same job.

Active Engagement

Ask the children to tell each other what they learned in this minilesson.

"Would you tell your partner two things you learned that you can do when you revise today and throughout the rest of your lives?"

Link

Send the children off with the reminder that some of them will add on to the ends and some to the middles of their stories.

"Writers, I heard so many of you say that today you will continue to reread your stories and think, 'What can I add to make this even better?' Some of you will add on to *the ends* of your stories, and you may need to get more sheets of paper to do that, and some of you will add in *the middles* of your stories. Some of you may invent whole *different* kinds of revision."

Reiterate that the children can use revision tools.

"Sometimes you won't have enough room, and if that happens, remember that writers use tools such as scissors and tape. If you are ready to work, thumbs up."

Because the minilesson is long, we keep the active-involvement time short. The specific requirement to tell each other two things energizes children's talk.

After children talk with their partners about what they learned, there is little to gain from having children report back—this often just drags everything out.

As often as possible, we end a minilesson by reminding children of the choices they have to make. For this reason, I let children know they may add on at the end or in the middle of their pieces. I also say, "Or you may invent a new idea." It is wise to give children opportunities to surprise us with their own inventions.

TIME TO CONFER

Be on the lookout for children who use tape and flaps (or invent a new ways) to add on to the middles of their drafts, because you may want one or two children to become exemplars for the day's share session. Also look for a child who adds on in a way that develops the main idea of the story. This child (and others who use other strategies worth highlighting) can be featured in future minilessons.

Whereas in the last session many of your conferences probably began with writers saying, "I'm done," or otherwise resisting revision, today you'll probably find that the prospect of using scissors and tape to add flaps is appealing enough that children work like eager beavers. The new tools will create new management issues, so give inspired mini-sermons about using their precious writing time well. See the conferences cited at right from the *Conferring with Primary Writers* book.

Use the conferring checklist today, because as you move among your children, you should already see evidence that they regard texts as malleable, using tools to elongate sections, and that they regard revision as a way to improve good writing.

Begin to preface your conferences with some variation of the question, "What are you working on as a writer?" Read the beginnings of many conference transcripts to see how we phrase this question. Notice how, in the conferences cited at right from the *Conferring with Primary Writers* book, we teach the child the sort of response we hope he or she will give us.

These conferences in *The Conferring Handbook* may be especially helpful today:

▶ *"This Part Is Confusing to Me"*
▶ *"Can You Reenact That Part In a Way That Shows Me How You Felt?"*
▶ *"Study an Example to Get Ideas for Revision"*

Also, if you have *Conferring with Primary Writers*, you may want to refer to the following conferences:

▶ "But How Did You Get There?!"
▶ "As a Reader, I'd Love to Hear More About That"
▶ "Make Sure You Are Adding Those Words for a Reason!"

Ask the writers to tell their partners not only *what* revision work they did—cutting, taping, adding on—but also *why*.

As partners talked about their revision, I listened in and jotted notes to myself. I was looking for a story to share with the rest of the class.

Rachel and Ted sat hip-to-hip in their writing nooks. Rachel read her piece. Pointing to the words, she'd added in purple ink, she said, "I revised by adding more words."

"Why'd you do that?"

"Because I wanted to say that I waited and waited at the table for my grandma. So I got revision paper and taped it on."

"I put paper in too!" said Ted. "I took a new piece of paper and put it in so that I could write a whole lot more about how I took the bus to get Alex to go to the Knicks game."

"We did the same thing!" both said excitedly.

When you eavesdrop on partners talking about their revisions, don't be surprised if they talk about adding a flap or inserting paper rather than talking about adding description or explanation. That is, their focus will be on the carpentry of revision, not the content.

- You may want to repeat this minilesson with slight variations. You may want to say, "I took your writing home last night, and I noticed that many of you added on. But what I noticed was that most of you added on to the ending of your papers." Then you could show the work of a few children who did that. "Sometimes, when writers only add on to the ending of a paper, it makes the story out of order and hard to follow." Read a draft from a previous year in which the writer wanted to expand an internal section but did so by sticking the new detail on at the end. "Did you hear how confusing that piece is? Today I'm going to teach you how writers add on in the middle of their drafts so their pieces make more sense." You could then show how the child fixed the problematic piece.

- Instead of making a flap, for added information, writers can cut a page in two and insert blank paper into the middle. Students can also learn to use an asterisk (or some other code). Some may take one page out of a book and replace it with several pages (or write a whole new book on just that one page). You don't need to illustrate each of these operations on each of the next five days—after a while you can teach three or four options, and the general principle, in a single minilesson. Alternatively, lure a child to use any of these methods for revision and then create a mid-workshop interruption in which you broadcast the child's "new" idea.

- Use your own writing to show an example of a similar revision or to demonstrate the process of revising, as you did in Session I.

You will probably find it impossible to resist rereading your children's work and enjoying their revisions. You can become a wiser teacher by nudging yourself to look at your children's work in ways that are new for you, and this unit's focus on process and strategies provides the perfect opportunity for you to deliberately look through new lenses. Reread the guiding questions in the following list and see if two or three of them work for you, and then let those questions alter your usual lens for looking at your students' work. The first five questions are organized in a gradient of complexity, with number five being the most rigorous. The final question is of a different kind and will launch some planning.

1. How much work did this writer seem to accomplish thus far during this unit of study? Is there evidence that the writer has been working with zeal?

2. What does the child tend to do in the name of revision?

3. Is there evidence that this child initiated revisions and did so without your support? Do you suspect the writer had peer support for this? Did he or she make these revisions totally independently?

4. Do the revisions improve the quality of the student's writing? Regardless of whether the revisions ultimately raise the level of a child's writing, does it seem to you the revisions grow out of an informed sense of what writers do and what constitutes good writing?

5. When writers revise, we usually use strategies (e.g., writing a new draft, adding a sentence) toward goals (for example, clarifying the reader's questions, showing feelings). Can you discern the qualities of good writing or goals this child aims toward in his or her revisions?

6. As you look over the children's narratives, what do you think the most substantive and helpful revisions could be? Imagine possible directions that might pay off.

ADDING DIALOGUE

GETTING READY

- Copy of *Owl Moon*, by Jane Yolen, or a similar text in which the dialogue adds to the story
- The shared story you have been working on with the class
- Sticky notes to add dialogue to the above piece
- Revision marker
- Revision folders containing writing pieces from previous session
- "Writers Revise" chart
- See CD-ROM for resources

SOME MINILESSONS ARE DESIGNED to *teach general concepts, and some equip children with particular strategies. In this minilesson, you will convey a general concept: Effective revisions come from using tools to accomplish goals.*

You will then proceed to teach one particular instance of this general concept. That is, after saying that writers add on for reasons (building suspense, developing the main idea, showing the internal story, developing the character, and so on), you will highlight one very concrete, straightforward reason to add to a draft. Sometimes writers add on to incorporate more dialogue. Today's particular goal—adding dialogue—is an easy one to teach and to learn. This is the first of many minilessons in which you will highlight the goals as well as the strategies for revision.

In this minilesson, you'll show writers how to add dialogue to their stories.

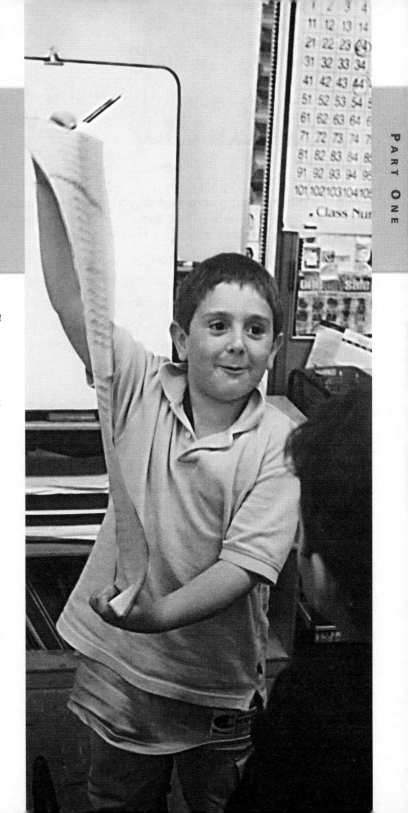

THE MINILESSON

Connection

Tell the children that you're glad they've been using tools to add on. Today you want to teach them that writers add on for purposes—and one such purpose is to make their characters express themselves (or talk).

"Writers, you all have been using tape and carats and new sheets of paper to add on to your writing, and that's great. Today I want to teach you that writers don't just add willy-nilly. We add for purposes. And one reason to add is that we decide to put the actual words a character says into a text. The actual words that a character says in a text are called *dialogue*."

Teaching

Cite a text the class knows well, and show that a bit of dialogue within that text adds to the story.

"Do you remember after the owl flapped its giant wings in *Owl Moon* and flew off, the characters decide to go home? Jane Yolen could have written, 'After that they went home.' But instead, she had the father talk to the child. Listen: '"Time to go home," Pa said to me.'" (I read this line with special expressiveness.) "'I knew then I could talk, I could even laugh out loud.' Just that tiny bit of dialogue really adds to the book."

I try to convey that writers revise to achieve particular purposes, by naming and dismissing the alternative. "We don't just add willy-nilly." Children love it when we use colorful language like this.

Notice that I use the word dialogue, *which the children have encountered before in their reading work. It is helpful to connect what children know as readers and what they know as writers.*

Here I rely on one of our touchstone texts to do the teaching. By doing so, I model for the children that published writers can be mentors for our own writing, a lesson that they can carry with them throughout their entire writing lives. Owl Moon *is a great text for showing the power of dialogue, because Yolen uses just a very few bits of dialogue. When children first incorporate dialogue into their drafts, they often overuse it, and their pieces are swamped with chit-chat—so choose a book in which dialogue is used sparingly.*

Active Engagement

Recruit the class to join you in adding dialogue to the shared story.

"I'm thinking we could add dialogue to our mouse story. Let me reread it, and will you think whether I could add the actual words someone said? Listen."

It was morning meeting.
Everyone heard a noise coming from the couch.
Patrick jumped up.
We saw there was a mouse under the cushion.
We thought it was a toy mouse. And then Pat started to pick it up but we screamed because it was a real mouse! It was tiny.

"Could you remember back to that day? Let's each of us think in our minds of the actual words someone said. Thumbs up when you've thought of something."

"Emma, would you come up and point to the place in this story where you'd have someone talk? Tell us the exact words you'd write. While she's coming up, would each of you be sure you know where *you'd* add the talk?"

Emma stood in front of the easel and pointed to the line in the story that said, "Patrick jumped up." "You could add, 'I heard it again,' 'cause that's what Patrick said."

"Okay, let me jot that on a sticky note and put it in the right place. Anything else?"

Romi said, "You should tell how Pat told us to listen to the story."

"What *exactly* did Pat say?" I asked. Explaining, I said, "I want to add, 'Then Pat said, "Such and such. . . ."'"

"I don't remember the exact way Pat said it."

The children are told up front why and how they are to listen as I read the story aloud.

It is helpful to make time for everyone to do this work mentally. When I say, "Thumbs up when you've thought of something," I am deliberately steering children away from raising their hands. I think thumbs up accomplishes the same job in a much less intrusive manner.

Often during interactive writing, while one child comes up to work with the text, everyone is encouraged to do something. I use this technique here, too, so that everyone will be thinking.

I use the sticky note to save time. The actual revisions happen later. Later, in the share, I show kids how to add dialogue using quotation marks.

Romi has named a problem many children face when writing dialogue: "I don't remember the exact way Pat said it," she worries. Children need to know that writers often don't remember the exact words and that we imagine the way the conversation probably went.

"You are smart to bring that up. We can just put down what Pat *probably* said. Writers often make up what someone probably said."

Romi thought for a minute. Then she said, "Maybe she said, 'Everyone, listen to the story. Forget that noise, it's nothing.'"

"Okay. And where would you put that?"

Romi showed the class where she would put that bit of dialogue. Using sticky note, I recorded her response and put it in the correct spot in the text.

Soon the story looked like this.

It was morning meeting.
Everyone heard a noise coming from the couch.
"Everyone, listen to the story," Pat said. "Forget that noise, it's nothing."
Patrick jumped up.
"I heard it again," he said.
We saw there was a mouse under the cushion.
We thought it was a toy mouse. And then Pat started to pick it up. We screamed because it was a real mouse!
It was tiny.

Link

Let the children know that their writing work today might include finding places in their story to include dialogue, then writing down the words that the characters said.

"Would you each get out the stories you are revising now and see if there is a place in that story where you might add dialogue? While you sit here on the rug, put a special code—maybe marks like this, " "—at that spot. Once you've found a place where you could add dialogue, you can get going. You may decide not to add dialogue, and that's okay, but reread and have a plan for today's revisions. Remember that you can revise in any of the ways we've listed on the 'Writers Revise' chart, or you can invent a new way. I'll be coming around to admire your work."

I seize this moment to teach a lesson that pertains not only to this moment and this piece but to the next session and to many future pieces.

Whenever I teach minilessons, children pose problems such as the one that arose in the middle of this minilesson, "What if I can't remember exactly what a person said, and I want to write dialogue?" Other times, the issues that children bring to a minilesson result in the lesson being more specific and more helpful than anything we'd planned to teach. But we need to be wary lest minilessons become maxilessons. I only entertain an issue with the whole-class minilesson if I believe it pertains to most children.

WRITERS REVISE

* We reread and make plans.

* We reread, make a movie in our minds, and add words.

* We add details to our drawings.

* We add missing information.

* We add dialogue.

MID-WORKSHOP TEACHING POINT

Intervene to tell the class about one child who revised in a new way. In this instance, highlight a child who revised *said*, substituting a more specific word. Then recruit the class to help the child revise a second *said* and suggest they might do likewise.

"Writers, may I stop all of you? Leo is adding dialogue to his draft, and he did a smart thing. He is describing how his little brother convinced his mom to stop for an ice cream cone. First Leo wrote, 'Rob *said*, "Can we please stop?"' Then he crossed out the word *said* and wrote *begged*. 'Rob *begged*, "Can we please stop?"' Then Leo wrote, '"No," Mom said.' Again he crossed out *said*. Leo and I have just now been thinking about how he could describe the way his mom said 'No.' Leo, show the kids how your mom spoke."

Leo spat out, "No."

"So what do you think? What word could Leo use instead of *said*?" I asked, and gave the class time to talk in partners. Soon we'd agreed that another alternative would be to say, "'No,' Mom snapped."

"It's good. I'll use it," Leo agreed.

"Writers, if you include dialogue, you might want to tell *how* the person talked, like Leo did. Did your character announce? Whisper? Add? Yell? See if you can find other ways to say *said*."

By gesturing to the chart, I model for the children that the chart is an ongoing resource for their revision work. Again, as the minilesson ends, they are reminded of choices before them in their writing work.

Some teachers decide to make each child a personal copy of a chart like this, or even turn the chart into a checklist and ask children to record when they've done things that are listed on the chart.

I quickly collect suggestions from the students. I don't want to take too long before the children get back to their writing work.

This mid-workshop advice amounts to almost a second minilesson and allows us to double the number of teaching points we make. Notice that the interruption contains many of the features of a minilesson.

TIME TO CONFER

In the minilesson, you told children that writers add for purposes and that one purpose might be to make characters talk—but there is no reason why every child needs to insert dialogue into their writing today! The truth is, unless your children are kindergartners or are struggling writers, they probably won't need your help adding dialogue anyhow. There will be plenty of other times when the minilesson requires follow-up in conferences. Take advantage of today! See the conferences cited at right. Use today's conferences to remind children that all the lessons you've ever taught are still pertinent. For example:

- Ask a child to check that readers can read the story well.
- Remind a child that it's important to take an extra minute to spell the words on the word wall correctly. "I can't believe it! You didn't take a second to spell the words you know just right! Gosh . . . do that now." Encourage the child to use known words to help them spell unfamiliar words.
- Notice that in the share after Session IV, you invite children to select a few more finished pieces that deserve revision. Some children will need permission to revise new pieces today.

 This conference in *The Conferring Handbook* may be especially helpful today:
- *"This Part Is Confusing to Me"*

Also, if you have *Conferring with Primary Writers*, you may want to refer to the following conferences:

- "As a Reader, I'd Love to Hear More About That"
- "Make Sure You Are Adding Those Words for a Reason"

AFTER-THE-WORKSHOP SHARE

Show the class the revisions you made to the shared story based on their input during the minilesson. Highlight the quotation marks.

"Writers, I took your suggestions and added the dialogue to our mouse story. Would you look at how I did this? What do you notice about the punctuation I used?" The children talked amongst themselves for a minute or two while I listened in on a couple of partnerships. When we reconvened, I explained the quotation marks (or talking marks).

"Some of you noticed these talking marks. They're actually called quotation marks, and they go around the exact words the character says. Like right here, Pat said, 'Everyone, listen to the story.' See how the marks go just around just those words because that's what came out of Pat's mouth? Then here Pat said, 'Forget that noise, it's nothing,' and again, the quotation marks go just around that because those words came out of her mouth. Quotation marks only go around the words the characters say in your stories. I bet lots of you will be adding quotation marks around the dialogue in your pieces."

Ask the children to show each other the revisions they've made thus far.

"Would you show your partner the revisions you made today? If you added dialogue, would you work together to make sure you use quotation marks in the right places?"

Notice that I use the share as a time to teach. The title— "share"—may be misleading because usually we have a teaching point in mind for this whole-group time, and often this teaching point extends the teaching point we made during the minilesson.

Alternatively, if share time is short, simply tell the story of the good work of one writer. Try to do this in a way that invites other writers to try the same thing. That is, we always want to send the message, "You, too, can do this." Be careful to make even your most struggling children famous during share time.

Usually when we teach anything, students over-learn what we teach. In the next session, you can expect to see pieces swamped in dialogue. Many children can initiate dialogue in their pieces, but they have a hard time letting the technique go. Often the entire piece becomes running commentary.

Remember that you are working with very young children. It is just fine if they overuse new language conventions. All is not lost when their pieces become worse, not better. When most of us try something new, we flounder a bit.

In school, we do everything we can to immerse all our children in richly literate lives. We read beautiful literature, provide wonderful books, share stories from our lives, and allow for lots of conversation. Then we ask them to do the work writers do, to add dialogue and all sorts of other good things to their drafts. Their first attempts may be messy or slightly off base, but we know children grow, in the fullness of time, as a result of repeated and steady support.

Study what your students are and are not doing. If they aren't yet adding dialogue into their drafts, teaching them about speech balloons should solve the problem. The more predictable problem will probably be that children overuse dialogue. If dialogue swamps some children's pieces entirely, copy a passage from your read-aloud book on to chart paper or use a big book, and point out how the author added just a bit of dialogue. This can be a minilesson or, alternatively, a small-group strategy lesson for the children needing this help.

REVISING BY TAKING AWAY

The ways we revise:
~ add where you are
~ make a new beginning
~ take away page when it doesn't make sense
~ show not tell
~ take away words that don't belong
~ add people talking or saying something
~ reread, cut and paste and staple
~ add pages
~ slow it down
~ tell what I saw
~ add details
~ add a new ending
~ change them into different things like poems, letters, directions, stories, notes, songs, how to do it.

I need help.

GETTING READY

- Shared story you've been revising, with some revisions you made at home in a contrasting color (be sure some of the revisions detract from the main point of the story)
- "Writers Revise" chart
- Writing folders containing writing from the previous units
- See CD-ROM for resources

WHEN YOU READ YOUR CHILDREN'S WRITING, *you'll probably see lots of evidence of flaps, arrows, and inserted pages. This will be heartening. It will be less heartening to read* their *revisions, especially if your children are first graders and if they have made a lot of revisions without your help (and subtle guidance). In these cases, a fair percentage of the revisions will have yielded pieces that are worse than* the *originals! This minilesson is an attempt to correct this problem. (It may not be necessary in kindergarten classrooms, where most of their revisions may have been ones you sponsored and may therefore improve rather than distract from the original draft.)*

Specifically, you'll teach children that revision can involve taking away from a draft as well as adding to it. You will emphasize that sometimes after we have revised by adding on to a text, we reread and decide our additions don't help after all. Then we take away—or, depending on your math curriculum, "We subtract!"

For example, if a child decides his story is about getting lost in the mall, and he wants to add dialogue, the dialogue that will help his story will be about getting lost/getting found ("'Did you see my mommy?' he asked," or "'Mommy!' he called"), not dialogue about being hungry en route to the shoe store ("'Can we go to McDonald's?'"). Your hope is to teach children that a writer needs to ask, "What is my story about?" and then to elaborate on aspects of the story that are central to its focus.

In this session, you'll teach children that revising also means taking away.

THE MINILESSON

Connection

Tell your children revisions can involve taking away as well as adding. Sometimes writers do both—they revise by adding and later realize their additions didn't help, so they decide to take away.

"Writers, you've learned that when we revise our writing, we often *add* to our stories," Pat began. "Today I am going to teach you that sometimes instead of *adding*, writers *take away* from a story. And *sometimes*, a writer does a lot of work adding details and *then* realizes, 'Oh, no! My additions didn't help.' And so the writer first adds and then takes stuff away. I know this first grader from last year who wrote a story about getting dressed up for her dance recital. When she revised it, she decided to add dialogue and details about her costume, getting ready, going to the recital, getting flowers after her performance, and going to Chuck E. Cheese's for dinner afterwards. She added so much stuff that she kind of lost the focus of her piece. But then, she did a really smart thing that writers do. She decided that all the additions didn't help, so she took some of them away. Today I will show you how you can ask, 'Should I take some things away?'"

Teaching

Teach the children to check to make sure their revisions elaborate on an important aspect of their story. Demonstrate how you test revisions you make. Show that sometimes you realize you have added peripheral information that detracts from your main point and that you can take away such things.

"You'll see that last night I added on to our mouse story. Notice the additions are in purple. Some of my additions help the story, and I'm thinking now, as I reread them, that some of them *don't* help the story. Let me read the new version aloud, and listen with me. Let's see if some of my revisions are helpful and some aren't helpful."

We often embed our teaching points into a story about one writer who did one thing, then the next thing, then the next thing. Pat tells the story of a writer who did a lot of work adding details and then realized, 'Oh, no! My additions didn't help.' And this writer had to take stuff away. Only after telling this little story does Pat say, "Today I will show you how you can ask, 'Should I take some things away?'"

Remember that your word choice can make your minilesson more memorable. Pat is wise to make her point using clean, parallel terms. She uses these terms consistently throughout the lesson and the whole unit. Writers can add—or take away.

Time and again you'll notice that we set children up early in the teaching section of a minilesson, so they know how to listen to whatever comes next.

It was morning meeting. **I had on my new sneakers. I wasn't hungry because I ate oatmeal for breakfast. Our classroom was quiet.** Everyone heard a noise coming from the couch. "Everyone, listen to the story," Pat said. "Forget that noise, it's nothing."

Patrick jumped up. "I heard it again," he said. **We lifted up the pillow. At first we saw nothing. Then in the corner** we saw a mouse under the cushion. We thought it was a toy mouse. And then Pat started to pick it up. We screamed because it was a real mouse! It was tiny.

"I'm trying to decide if some parts aren't helpful. Umm . . . watch how I do this. I'm thinking, 'What is the most important idea in my story? What is my story really about?' Umm . . . I want it to be about finding a mouse in our sofa during read-aloud and how we screamed. So now I have to see if I added some things that don't go with what the story is mainly about. Umm. . . ."

Active Engagement

Ask the children to help you judge whether your revisions built on the main idea. Some revisions will have helped; some will not have helped.

"Will you all help me? Tell your partner if you see sections of the text that aren't about the main idea of the story."

Pat listened in on what partners were saying to each other. She was listening for evidence of both understanding and confusion. After a bit, Pat called on a few children, including some whose comments she'd heard as they did their partner shares.

"I don't think the sneakers go in this story."

"Or the part about oatmeal, 'cause you are not going to put the whole day, your whole life in your story!"

"Or your story will be a junk pile."

The content of this minilesson is probably more complicated than that of any other minilesson this year. Even adult writers struggle with the concept you are trying to teach today. You'll make your point without subtlety so that your children are more apt to understand—and because they'll only employ this concept in nonsubtle ways.

Pat doesn't just summarize the fact that she rereads, searching for what is and isn't essential to the text. She reenacts doing this reading. The difference is an essential one. Be prepared to role-play. Steer clear of a lot of explanations about how you review. Just do it, don't talk about it.

Reiterate the larger lesson that you hope children take with them, and add it to your ongoing "Writers Revise" chart.

"You know, as I reread my story, I think you are right. So I'll cross out these lines about the oatmeal and sneakers. Writers revise by *subtracting* as well as by adding, don't we? Let's add this to the 'Writers Revise' chart."

WRITERS REVISE

* We reread and make plans.
* We reread, make a movie in our minds, and add words.
* We add details to our drawings.
* We add missing information.
* We add dialogue.
* We subtract things that don't build our main idea.

The rhythm in a minilesson is that we name what we will teach. We set children up to be ready to observe or otherwise learn from what we say or do. Then we explain or demonstrate. Then we reiterate what we hope students have learned that they can, we trust, take with them to another day and another piece.

Ask children to be sure their revisions *add to* their pieces.

"I know you will use our 'Writers Revise' chart and revise in lots of ways today. But before you get started doing other revisions, will all of you look back on the revisions you've made over the past few days and see if you have parts like I had (like the ones about the sneakers and the oatmeal), that don't go with the main thing in the story? And any time you see your writing has parts that don't help, remember that writers take away as well as add. Get started rereading right here, and when you feel certain you know what to do, you can go to your writing spots."

MID-WORKSHOP TEACHING POINT

If you see a discarded draft, call this to everyone's attention and then publicly rescue the draft and make a fuss about saving precious revisions.

"Guess what? I found a draft in the trash can! I'm so surprised, because I want to see and save all your precious revisions. Don't throw anything away!"

When children revise, they will throw pieces of paper away and start afresh. They need to understand that these pieces might still be used later (and your celebration at the end of the unit will highlight rejected attempts and discarded drafts). So encourage children to save all of their work in their folders.

TIME TO CONFER

Today's minilesson is at the heart of this unit of study. Over and over in this unit, you will help children revise in ways that develop the main aspect of their narratives. This is very sophisticated for young children, and they won't all "get it," even after you teach this fairly extensively. Almost half your conferences in this unit will support today's minilesson. Study the conference cited at right as one good example. You'll notice that the conference has several sections. It's predictable that first the writer determines what he or she is trying to show in the story, then the writer decides where he or she conveys that main idea, and finally, the writer develops that section of the story. See also the conference cited at right from the *Conferring With Primary Writers* book.

Meanwhile, you will want to use your conferring chart to record what children are self-initiating, what they seem almost able to do, and what you are teaching.

 This conference in *The Conferring Handbook* may be especially helpful today:

> ▶ *"Can You Reenact That Part in a Way That Shows Me How You Felt?"*

Also, if you have *Conferring with Primary Writers*, you may want to refer to the following conference:

▶ "Can You Reenact That Part in a Way That Shows Me Exactly What Happened?"

AFTER-THE-WORKSHOP SHARE

Suggest that the children locate other pieces that are worthy of being revised and add these to their revision folders.

"Some of you have finished revising the piece you published at our previous Celebration Day. If that piece is as good as you can make it, go back to your writing folder and choose three other stories that you think deserve to be revised and move them to your revision folder. You can start revising those pieces. You can revise using all the strategies we've learned. Take a few minutes to select those deserving pieces now and to move them into your revision folder." [*Fig. IV-1*]

Throughout this unit, Pat scaffolds the children's management of their pieces of writing. Her expectation is that all children will revise several pieces in the course of this revision study.

I went up in my grandma's attic. I found the doll. It was special to my mom loved this doll. It was in the attic.

I gave my grandma a hug for getting my mom's favorite doll. I did the doll a manicure.

Fig. IV-I Carly decided she would work on her favorite piece.

IF CHILDREN NEED MORE TIME

You will probably want to do a version of this minilesson in small-group strategy lessons. For tomorrow's minilesson, move on to Session V, but after that and often throughout the year, revisit the topic of today's minilesson.

▸ Tell children that Jane Yolen based the book *Owl Moon* on the true story of how her husband and her sons often traipsed into the woods together. But the true story of traipsing through the woods probably involved finding mittens, turning off the television, telling the dog he couldn't come, jokes they told along the way, and a million other things Jane decided to leave out. "She only added the things that went with the main idea, and the main feeling, of her story," you could say. "I'm going to read bits of her book, and I want you to think what Jane decided was the main thing she wanted to show! 'Our feet crunched over the crisp snow . . . I could feel the cold, as if someone's icy hand was palm-down on my back . . . I listened and looked so hard my ears hurt and my eyes got cloudy with the cold. . . .' Turn and tell your partner, 'What was the main thing Jane Yolen seems to have been trying to show?'" (You can substitute almost any well-written, well-loved book that the class knows well.)

▸ Give your children lots of practice angling their stories to make a point, because this is fundamental. If your class hamster gets loose, for example, ask children to turn to their partners and retell the story in a way that really shows how worried they were. Get them started by saying a bit of dialogue, such as, "'Where is he?' Mark asked, and we all hurried over. We looked in the cage. . . ." Then, ask children to think about the same episode only this time, to tell the story in a way that shows how proud they are of their smart, smart hamster. Again, get them started, perhaps using the exact same words, "'Where is he?' Mark asked." (Obviously you'll need to reshape this example to fit your own class.)

PLANNING REVISION

GETTING READY

- Three stories that deserve to be revised in everyone's revision folder
- Several large, blank sticky notes placed on each of the to-be-revised stories
- A new, very sparse Small-Moment story about a topic the children know; write this at home on a chart paper booklet
- Sticky notes, ready for making revision plans to the above story
- "Writers Revise" chart and checklists
- See CD-ROM for resources

THIS MINILESSON SIGNALS AN IMPORTANT BEND in the road. For the first week or so, each child revised one previously published piece. Now they've brought a few more texts that "deserve to be revised" into their revision folder, and this will galvanize them with new energy. The revision workshop will suddenly feel like it is flooded with stories, each calling out to be revised. This is a good opportunity, then, to nudge children to do the rereading and assessing that's so crucial to revision.

Revision isn't just about adding on or taking away. It is also about re-vision, or seeing again. How important it is to promote reflection and self-assessment! With young children, we teachers sometimes do all the rereading and assessing, and children merely follow our marching orders. This means we end up doing much of the work (and the learning).

In this minilesson, you'll encourage children to reread their pieces, thinking, "What's good in these stories that especially deserves to be built on?" The wording in that question is important, because you are still helping children realize that revisions are not corrections for mess-ups. Writers also think, "What problems do I see that especially call out for attention?" or "What's not so good that I can fix?"

In this session, you'll encourage children to reread, assess, and make plans for revising the new pieces they've brought into their revision folders.

Connection

Remind the children that their revision folders contain work that needs their attention.

"At the end of yesterday's workshop you each selected a few stories that deserve to be revised. You put them in your revision folder. This is an exciting day, because we have so much new material. It's as if we are artists, and today we have all these new canvasses and new clay."

Teach the children that, above all, revision means *re-vision*, to see again.

"Writers, today I want to teach you what the word *revision* really means. There are two parts to the word. There is the *re* part, and the *vision* part. Vision means *to see*. You go to an eye doctor to check your vision, what you see. If your vision needs help, you get glasses.

"*Re* always means to do again. If you reheat pizza, you heat it again. And *re*-vision means you see your writing again. You might have thought revision meant fixing up your writing. But really, the most important thing you do when you revise your writing is that you look at it again."

At this point, Pat joined me at the front of the meeting area. She was carrying her revision folder. Although the children didn't know it yet, her folder contained a piece she'd written on a three-page booklet made of chart paper. "Today, Pat and I will teach you how we look over our writing, how we see it again."

Teaching

Model thoughtful ways to reread writing.

"Like you, Pat looked through her writing and found some of her old stories that seem special enough to revise, and her stories, like yours, are in her revision folder. So she'll show you how she rereads. You be researchers and notice what she does."

In this connection, I say, "Writers, today I want to teach you what the word 'revision' really means." In every connection, you should see the teacher come out and say, "Today I will teach you. . . ." Oftentimes what teachers tend to do instead is say, "Writers, today we will do (such and such)." This is a clue that instead of teaching, the teacher may be assigning. In that case, it's time to restructure the minilesson.

This minilesson involves both of us—I comment on Pat's work. Many times teachers will orchestrate similar minilessons using a student teacher or a paraprofessional as the partner in the reenactment. Before Pat reenacts or reads aloud, we set the children up to know what they are watching for.

Role-playing the part of a writer who rereads her own work, Pat read her draft quietly to herself, but loud enough for the class to hear: "'We went to the garden to catch fish.' Hmm. Who is 'we'? I should explain that more." She again read aloud to herself. "'We went to the garden to catch fish.'"

"It sounds as if we try to catch fish in the grass. I should say there was a pond in the garden." Pat jotted the word *explain* on a sticky note tag, and left it at the appropriate spot on the draft. "I'm going to put a sticky note here that says *explain*, to help me remember to do this. Okay, I'm going to keep rereading. 'I tried to catch a fish.' I should add on to this part. I could write about the net we taped together to try to catch fish." Pat jotted another note, *add on*, and again left it at the appropriate spot. "'I couldn't catch any fish. Mrs. Rosen tried and caught three fish.' I could say more about Mrs. Rosen and how she showed up with her fishing rod, her yellow knee-high boots, and her can of bait." Now Pat wrote the word *show* on a sticky note tag and left it on the draft. "'We went back to our classroom.' That's okay."

Active Engagement

Have the children discuss with partners what they noticed about how the adult writer reread his or her writing. Elicit a few responses.

I said to the students, "Will you turn and tell your partner what you saw Pat doing when she reread?"

Pat and I listened in on partners' conversations, then convened the group. "What did you notice, Eric?" I asked.

"Pat wrote on sticky notes."

"Class, listen to what I'm going to ask Eric, because it applies to you, too. Earlier, Eric, I asked, 'What did you see Pat doing?' and you pointed out that Pat wrote on sticky notes. That's true. But listen to what I'm going to suggest. Eric, when I ask you to be a researcher and to notice what Pat or someone else does, you need to retell what you see in order—like we retell our small moments in order. Can you say what Pat did first, then next, then next? What did Pat do *first*?"

"First she read it."

Pat has written a Small Moment story, like the stories she's asking her children to write, and it's about an episode the children are familiar with.

Keep your story very short. If it is too long or too intriguing, your teaching point can get lost in the detail.

Notice that within a five-line story, Pat has shown four different reasons to revise. The advantage of using our own writing in minilessons is we can "make it to order."

When Eric describes what he saw a writer do, he is doing something he and others will do countless times during his elementary school years. It is worth intervening to lift the level of anything that will become an ongoing ritual. In this instance, if Eric learns to sequentially retell what Pat did as a writer, he is practicing learning to tell and write narratives. The class has worked hard to learn this while writing these Small Moment stories.

"That's true, isn't it? She did reread her draft. And she didn't read it like this," I said and acted out a perfunctory, glancing-at-a-text sort of reading, "did she?"

"No. She took her time and read every word," Eric agreed.

"Then she wrote on the paper," Emma added.

"Yes," I said, rephrasing Emma's comment to make it more specific. "She first reread her draft, then she jotted plans about things she'd like to revise."

Link

Send the children off to their revision work. A few may still be revising their first piece, but most will be working on a second piece from their revision folders.

"I know some of you are almost done revising your first piece and others are starting to revise new pieces. When it comes time to revise a new piece, would you first reread and make plans? I'll admire your planning."

"Thumbs up if you are almost done revising your first piece. Okay. Off you go. The rest of you, would you start revising by *rereading and making revision* plans on the sticky note tags you'll find on your pieces? Then you can get started revising those pieces. Okay? Off you go."

MID-WORKSHOP TEACHING POINT

Intervene to ask each writer to articulate to his or her partner what he or she plans to do in the name of revision.

"May I stop everyone just for a minute or two? I want you to tell your partners what your plans for revision are today. Listen to each other's plans, and make sure your partners have sticky notes in place to remind them of the revisions they want to make."

When I want to highlight the fact that Pat read her draft in a thoughtful, deliberate way, I act out what she did not do, as well as what she did do.

WRITERS REVISE

- We reread and make plans.
- We reread, make a movie in our minds, and add words.
- We add details to our drawings.
- We add missing information.
- We add dialogue.
- We subtract things that don't build our main idea.

This chart grows out of a sequence of days, not just one. It's nice when there is a concrete way to show that one day's minilesson develops what has been taught on previous days. Notice, however, that adding on to the chart is not the essence of the minilesson day after day.

We need to anticipate that not all children will move lockstep through the workshop. The content of many minilessons won't apply to every child on the same day, because children will be in different places on any given day.

I keep the children who are just starting to revise on the carpet. This gives me a chance to ensure they translate my directions into actions. I sit among them, sending children off as I see evidence that they are rereading and jotting revision plans.

Until now, when children talk with each other about writing, they usually talk about their subject or fulfill a particular assignment ("Can you find places to add dialogue?"). This partnership share helps children get used to the sort of talk writers do a lot, rather like the talk in a peer conference. The writer will tell the partner what he or she has done and plans to do.

Be on the lookout for a child whose leads sound like captions. You may want to encourage this child to leave a sticky note tag saying, "fix lead," so you can use this child in tomorrow's minilesson. See the conferences cited at right.

So far, you've taught children to regard their drafts as malleable, and to use tools (scissors, tape, staples) to move around bits of text.

You also want to teach children to become more deliberate writers. Revision provides an opportunity to teach writers to act in purposeful ways. It is a stretch to think that most six-year-olds could pause for example, before launching a first draft, and think, "I'll bring out my characters by having them talk." On the other hand, it is entirely reasonable to think that a six-year-old can reread a finished draft and say, "I'm going to revise by having my characters talk, adding speech balloons into the picture or even dialogue into the text."

To assess and encourage children's growing deliberateness as writers, you'll want to interview your children as they embark on revisions. "What are you trying to do?" you'll ask over and over. "How will you do that?"

Children will say what you've said to them: that they are adding dialogue, for example, or details. Your hope is that you'll see children approaching their pieces with goals that come from rereading and from thinking, "What would make this draft even better?" When a child generates his own plans from assessing a draft, celebrate this initiative whether or not you agree with the child's direction.

When children have energy and initiative, conferring needn't propel them, but can, instead, guide them. Today, then, make a point to support independence and initiative. Sit at a table of writers, clipboard in hand, recording their doings. Let them know you are noting their smart decisions. They'll work zealously if they see you watching, and your research will actually be a fabulous way to teach independence and initiative.

This conference in *The Conferring Handbook* may be especially helpful today:

- ▶ *"Study an Example to Get Ideas for Revision"*

Also, if you have *Conferring with Primary Writers*, you may want to refer to the following conference:

- ▶ "Are All of Your Words Important to Your Story?"

Give the children a checklist version of the "Writers Revise" chart, one for each revised piece, and ask them to check off the revision strategies they used for each piece.

"Writers, would you get with your partners again? And put all the pieces you've revised in front of you? Do that now, then give me your eyes to show me that you are ready."

"Today we learned that writers stop to reread and think and that this helps us have new plans for revision. One way to do that is to look at our work and then to look at our 'Writers Revise' charts and say, 'Which of these things have I done with this piece?' Let's use the chart to think about our mouse story."

"Later, I'll give each of you one personal copy of our 'Writers Revise' chart for each of your revised stories. Write the title of your story up here on the top of the chart, like I will write *A Mouse*, then you'll do like this. . . .'" On a large version of the "Writers Revise" checklist, I showed the children how to fill it in.

"Let's see. 'We reread and make plans.' We didn't do that on this story, did we? So I'll check no. Let's continue. I definitely remember making a movie in my mind of the mouse. We did that over and over, so I'll check yes. Let's keep reading."

The charts that you and the class make over the course of a unit of study outline your hopes for children. It makes sense, then, to turn these charts over to children. Why not give children personal copies of most wall charts, and why not encourage them to keep track of the extent to which they've done whatever is listed on the chart?

STORY TITLE: A MOUSE

Strategy	Yes	No
We reread and make plans.		✔
We reread, make a movie in our minds, and add words.	✔	

"'We add details to our drawings.' Let's see if we did that." I looked closely at the illustrations. "Yes, we did that here . . . and here's another place where I added detail . . . so I'll check yes. Now we'll need to read the next three things on our list and decide if we've done them, and then we can check yes or no."

STORY TITLE: A MOUSE

Strategy	Yes	No
We reread and make plans.		✔
We reread, make a movie in our minds, and add words.	✔	
We add details to our drawings.	✔	
We add missing information.		
We add dialogue.		
We subtract things that don't build our main idea.		

"Writers, the reason you fill in the chart is that you might find you haven't done one of these things, and then you and your partner will want to think, 'If I did this thing, would it improve my piece? Should I turn that item on the chart into a revision plan for my piece?' If so, leave yourself a sticky note with your plan jotted on it."

"So turn to your writing now, and for each piece, fill out one of these charts. You can do this alone or with your partner. When you've finished with a chart, paper-clip it to your story, okay?"

Remember that usually when you are unsure what, exactly, to teach, the best answer is that you need to teach children the process of doing something that you hope they'll do later on their own.

You may want to look over your children's charts and their work, noticing what strategies you (and they) think they have and haven't used. The most challenging strategy for children to initiate themselves will be taking away material from their stories. You may decide, therefore, to point this out and to challenge them to do this—or you may just let that strategy go.

As you reread and assess their pieces, one of the questions you'll ask is, "What revision strategies and what qualities of writing could I teach next that might have a special payoff for these kids?"

The answer to this question will vary, depending a lot on the success of your original Small-Moment unit. If children left that unit writing pieces that weren't focused, sequential, Small-Moment narratives, then you may want to design minilessons that reteach the basic concepts of Small-Moments writing. In the name of revision, you could do new versions of any of the minilessons you taught in that unit. Look especially at Sessions II, VII, and XI.

Notice, too, whether your children are writing in the voice of a storyteller instead of summarizing events. There is a world of difference between the two voices:

A Storyteller's Voice:	A Summarizing Voice:
Bingo barked at me. "You want to play Frisbee?" I asked and she barked again. I backed way up and threw the Frisbee. It flew over Bingo's head.	Bingo likes to play Frisbee. She barks until I throw it at her. Sometimes she catches it. I throw it over her head a lot.

Revising a story to bring out a storyteller's voice requires at least a new lead—and often a new draft.

REVISING LEADS

GETTING READY

- Sample piece of writing (a child's or your own) where the lead has been revised
- *A Chair for My Mother*, by Vera B. Williams, *Owl Moon*, by Jane Yolen, or other familiar books with great leads
- See CD-ROM for resources

YOUR REVIEW OF YOUR CHILDREN'S WRITING *will no doubt suggest that many of them could profit from some attention to leads. Quite a few of their leads probably sound like captions for illustrations rather than story openings. A number of Pat's children began each piece like this: "This is me at the park." "Here I am. . . ." Other children summarized rather than retold events. For example, one child began, "I go to the park a lot and sometimes. . . ." This minilesson, then, is designed to give children strategies for revising their leads.*

The challenge in planning a minilesson like this is that you need to understand what your children are currently doing (and trying to do) when they write leads, so that you can put your finger on something you could teach that would really help. There are a zillion things you could say about effective leads, and you need to choose among them.

You might think about your own writing process and try to articulate how you go about generating leads. Contrast this with the processes you believe your children are probably using. This may help.

You could also look at leads in books your children already know and love, and try to name how those leads are fundamentally different from what you see in many of your children's stories.

It was this sort of process that led us to design this minilesson, which will raise children's awareness and knowledge of effective leads and nudge them to include rewriting one's lead as part of their revision process.

THE MINILESSON

Connection

Point out that in their revision plans, many children decided to improve their leads, and today you'll show them how to do this.

"Yesterday, many of you reread your writing and made revision plans. And some of you, like Eric, wrote, 'One. Fix lead.' Eric has three leads from his folder that he wants to fix. They go like this." [*Fig. VI-1*]

"So I thought today we'd study how authors write great leads, and then we'd try to write like those authors."

Teaching

Tell the children that just as they often learn from experts in sports, today they'll study an expert writer.

"Have you ever wanted to learn to do something in sports—like throw a Frisbee, or do a yoyo trick—and then *watched the experts* to figure out what *they're* doing? Let's do that now. Because we want to learn how to write great leads, let's look at what some of the authors we know do to start a great story."

I read three of Eric's leads because I suspect this will help children see the patterns across the leads enough to notice the way that Eric's leads are different from those in the stories they read. It is very helpful to read pieces that are similar, yet not the same.

This is me when I lost a tooth at the park on a nice day.

This is me when I had a parade in my school. I had so much fun in the parade. We wore our costumes.

This is me when I scored my first basket in basketball. The other team frowned. My team scored. I put my hand up and screamed, "Yeah!"

Fig. V1-1　Eric

Ask the children to listen as you read and then reread the lead from a familiar book. Set them up to be ready to say what the author has done to write this lead.

"Let's look at *A Chair for My Mother*, by Vera B. Williams. You remember the main thing at the start of the book is that the little girl collects coins in the big green jar. Listen to Vera's lead. Will you think, 'How is she starting her story?'"

> My mother works as a waitress in the Blue Tile Diner. After school I meet her there. Then her boss, Josephine, gives me a job too. I wash the salts and peppers and fill the ketchups. One time I peeled all the onions for onion soup. When I finish, Josephine says "Good work, honey" and pays me. And every time, I put half of my money into the jar.

"I'm going to read this lead again, and let's all think really hard about what Vera does to start her story so maybe we'll get ideas for how we can start our stories." I reread the lead. "Would you turn and talk with your partner about what Vera B. Williams does that we could do in our stories?"

After partners tell each other what they notice, gather a few of their observations.

"So, what are you saying? Heather?"

"She tells about the salt."

"Uh huh . . ."

"She tells little details," Heather said.

"Can you give examples?"

"She washes the salt and pepper things."

"Do the rest of you agree with Heather's observation that Vera starts her story by writing details?"

"Yeah, 'cause it tells the name of the store."

When I use literature to teach a particular technique, I usually revisit books children know well. I remind children of the book's contents so I'm not asking them to consider a passage totally out of context.

Rereading is an incredibly valuable activity, especially for writers who want to study how an author has constructed a text. We read to what a text says, and then listen again thinking about the techniques the author has used. When we reread a text, we can listen with an ear toward technique.

Because we want children to elaborate on their first thoughts when they write about their lives and about texts other authors have written, we nudge children to elaborate on their first thoughts when they talk about texts. When you elicit observations from a member of the class, scaffold and nudge so the child provides supporting details. Allow yourself to extend what one or two children say rather than feeling pressured to call on lots of kids.

Notice how I sustain this one exchange instead of jumping to new children.

When I involve new children, I do so by asking them to extend the current line of conversation.

Reiterate and clarify what the author has done that you hope children emulate when they write their leads.

"Writers, I think you are on to something. Vera Williams doesn't just say, 'Here I am at my mother's job. Sometimes I help out and get money for it,' does she? She tells us *exactly* where she is and what she is doing—she starts right in with a very detailed action story. Right in the first lines, she says, 'I wash the salt and pepper shakers and fill the ketchups.'"

"Let's look at another lead. Listen to the lead in Jane Yolen's *Owl Moon*. The book starts like this."

> It was late one winter night,
> long past my bedtime,
> when Pa and I went owling.
> There was no wind.
> The trees stood still
> as giant statues.

"Tell your partner what you noticed!"

As children share, listen in on their conversations. Again, name what you heard a child or two say that will be helpful for others.

"Writers, I'm hearing you say that she writes with pretty, songlike words: 'It was late one winter night . . . There was no wind. The trees stood still as giant statues.' And Emma pointed out that she *shows* the weather. It's funny that Emma noticed that, because once I had a writing teacher who told me, 'If you aren't sure how to start a story, show the weather. Say, "The skies were turning gray when I left for my grandma's" or "It was so cold I could see my breath when I went to the movies."'"

Active Engagement

Use one student's piece of writing and ask the class to help this student revise his lead.

"Writers, we saw that instead of saying, 'My mom works. I go to her job,' Vera has told about how as a little girl, she washed the salt and pepper shakers. Writers do that sometimes—we write with tiny details. And writers also do like Jane Yolen and sometimes show the weather. Would you and your partner listen while I reread the lead to one of Eric's stories, and then will you borrow either Vera Williams's or Jane Yolen's strategies, and see if you can come up with a

To dramatize what Vera Williams does, I juxtapose it with what she doesn't do. ("Vera doesn't say, 'Here I am at my mother's job.'") I emphasize that Vera starts by telling a very detailed action. This is an effective way to start a story.

I am returning to the same books I've used often, and looking at them in new ways. Children can attend to an author's technique in a book they know well more easily than they can in a new book, where their attention is usually diverted to plot. Notice also that we almost never read an entire book in a minilesson. If our point is to highlight the leads authors have written, we will make our point better by looking at the leads of several texts rather than by looking all the way through any one text.

The advice to start with the weather caught on like wildfire in Pat's room and soon spread to zillions of New York City classrooms, giving a new literary feel to children's texts. A piece that began, "One time I went roller skating," is transformed by the weather, "One bright sunny day I went roller skating."

Make sure to ask the student ahead of time if it is okay to use his or her work as an example. Be sure that the student doesn't regard this as remedial. After all, you often ask students to help you with your writing!

suggestion for Eric? Eric started his story about our Halloween parade, saying, 'This is me when I had a parade in school.' You remember our Halloween parade. If Eric was going to revise his lead and start by telling a tiny detail, what could he say? Tell your partner."

"Do you remember the thunderstorm during our parade? If Eric wanted to revise his lead and say, 'It was such-and-such a kind of day' and then get to the parade part, what could he say about the weather?"

Link

Remind the students of the lessons they should have learned.

"Today, I know some of you will be reworking your leads. If you are fixing your lead, you might do these things."

To Write a Strong Lead

▸ Write with detail.
▸ Show the weather.
▸ Make it sound like a song.

"You might also look again at other books and notice other good ideas. How many of you have plans for what you'll be doing today? Okay, off you go."

This minilesson has been long enough already. It isn't necessary to hear back from children. They've had a chance to practice revising a lead—that's valuable. Now it's time for these writers to write.

For now, merely say this aloud. Tonight you can make a chart, but don't slow the minilesson down now.

TIME TO CONFER

To give today's minilesson power, you'll probably tailor half your conferences so they support the lesson. For these conferences, you may want to confer with a children's book in hand. Choose a book the students know well, and be ready to suggest that the author could have started the book in a bland fashion, and then invent a description of what the writer probably did to get a better lead. Imagine the author did whatever you hope this child will now do to write a great lead.

If you can confer with a handful of children to help them revise their leads, another half a dozen children will pick up on this just by eavesdropping (especially if you encourage this). See the conferences cited at right.

Meanwhile, however, you'll want your other conferences to help children continue to move along lines of growth. Perhaps you have been working to support one child's stamina and another child's ability to use what she knows of word endings to spell. These conferences should come from your sense of each writer and the work he or she needs to do next.

 This conference in *The Conferring Handbook* may be especially helpful today:

▶ *"Study an Example to Get Ideas for Revision"*

Also, if you have **Conferring with Primary Writers**, you may want to refer to the following conference:

▶ "Let's Look at Your Lead and Your Ending"

Point out that it's satisfying to look between draft one and draft two.

"In my house, we have a giraffe on our wall that has measurements alongside it, showing three feet, four feet, five feet, and all the inches in between. Often Miles and Evan stand alongside the measuring stick and we mark how tall they've gotten to be—and then we look back on how tall they used to be and we say, 'Wow, you've grown!' Writers grow too, and we can look back on our growth by comparing our first draft and our revised draft. With your partners today, will those of you who revised your lead share your first lead, and then share your revised lead? If you've done other revisions, share the first version and the new version. Admire the ways in which your writing or your partner's writing has grown 'taller.'"

The room erupted into a hubbub of conversation and reading aloud. I listened in on a few partnerships and quickly reconvened the class.

"Listen to Eric's first lead—and to his revised lead. Let's see how much this writer has grown!" First version [*Fig. VI-2*]: "This is me when I lost a tooth at the park on a nice day." Second version [*Fig. VI-3*]: "It was a hot summer day. I was in the park practicing my bike. When I got tired, I wiggled my tooth, it didn't come out. I pulled my tooth, it came out easy."

Name: Eric

This is me win I Lost A towt At The prk On A Niys Day

This is me when I lost a tooth at the park on a nice day.

Fig. VI-2   Eric

it WAS A Hit SAMr DAY I WAS IN The PArk PrAtsRN My Biek WiN I Git tiYD I WAGLD MY ToWt it DADNt CAM QUt I PLD MY TOWt it cAm out siriSy

It was a hot summer day. I was in the park practicing my bike. When I got tired, I wiggled my tooth, it didn't come out. I pulled my tooth, it came out easy.

Fig. VI-3   Eric

‣ Repeat the same minilesson, using other examples of familiar children's literature. You may want to select texts that start in similar ways (*The Paperboy*, by Dave Pilkey, for example, is similar to *Owl Moon*).

‣ Show other ways to start a story—many authors, for example, start their stories by introducing characters. Often they list a few things about a character (see Patricia Polacco's *My Rotten Redheaded Older Brother*, or Mary Hoffman's *Amazing Grace*).

‣ Confer with a child to help him or her try a new lead, and then use that child's first and revised lead as an example. This can be very powerful, because the leads you're apt to show from published children's books will be well beyond anything the children could write.

‣ Help children brainstorm different techniques for starting a story, and then try each of these variations on the same story about something the class experienced together. For example, Pat and her children could have begun their story of the mouse with references to the weather, as in *Owl Moon*: "It was a sparkling fall day. The crisp, clean air felt good. Little did we know what was lurking in our classroom." They could have begun the same story with details about the place, such as those Vera B. Williams used: "Each morning we sat in the library corner of our classroom. It's the most special spot in our room, full of books and couches and chairs. The green couch is the throne, the most special place of all. We got the couch from Pat. It has a few holes in it, but it still is our favorite place." Alternatively, the mouse story could have begun with dialogue. "'What's all the noise about?' Pat asked her class. 'RUN!' shouted Patrick. 'THERE'S A MOUSE INSIDE OUR COUCH!!!'"

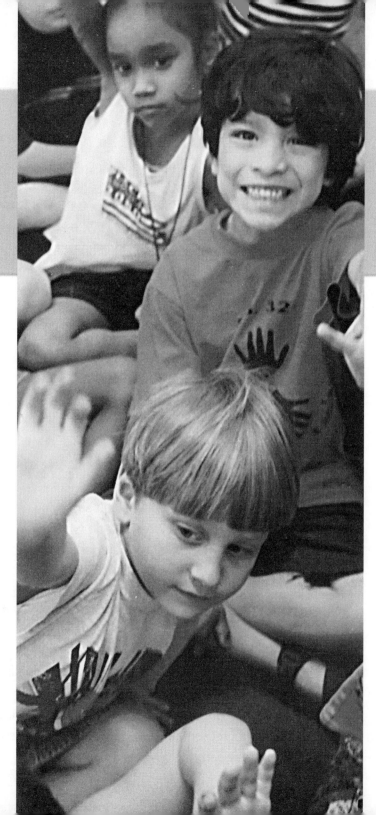

TEACHING CHILDREN TO CONFER ABOUT WRITING

GETTING READY

▸ Child willing to role-play
▸ Piece of writing to use as a prop in the role play
◉ See CD-ROM for resources

THIS MINILESSON TEACHES A SKILL: *What the writer's job is in a writing conference.*

Specifically, you'll teach children to anticipate that writing conferences begin with the question "What are you working on as a writer?" You want children to know that the appropriate answer includes not just the child's subject ("my dog") but also the child's writing plans ("I'm trying to help you picture my dog").

When children answer the question "What are you working on as a writer?" the words they use don't emerge out of the clear blue sky. Instead, children say back the words and strategies we've taught them. At this time in the year and in this unit, we can expect them to say, "I'm revising my lead" or "I'm adding dialogue" or "I'm showing the weather" or "I'm adding detail." This, then, is a perfect time to teach children their roles in writing conferences.

Then, too, children need some requisite knowledge before this particular minilesson will be within their reach. You may decide to reserve this minilesson for first and second grades.

In this session, you'll teach children to answer the question "What are you working on as a writer?" by describing not only the content of their writing but also their plans for what they are working on as writers.

THE MINILESSON

Connection

Tell the children that you will teach them what their jobs are in revision conferences.

"Writers, ever since the start of the year, during each day's writing workshop, you've seen me come around and confer with you about your writing. When I confer with you, I have a job that I'm doing. But *you* also have a job in these conferences, and I'm not sure you know your job. Today I want to teach you what your job is in a writing conference."

Teaching

Tell your students the structure of a conference.

"I don't know if you realize it or not, but every time I confer, I always start by doing the same things."

"First, I watch. You'll see me draw a chair near to you. Usually I don't say anything for a few minutes. I'm watching what you do as a writer—and your job during this first part of a conference is to keep doing what you do as a writer. Don't stop because I'm close. Don't say, 'May I read my piece to you?' Keep working so I can watch what you do when you write."

"Then next, I usually ask a question. I might ask, 'What are you doing as a writer?' or 'What are you working on?'"

Now tell your students their main job in a conference. Demonstrate what they often do—contrasting this with a demonstration of what you'd prefer they do in conferences.

"This is the time when you have a big job. Let me show you what you sometimes do—and what I wish you'd do. You all be researchers and notice the difference. Omid has said he'll be the teacher, I'll be the writer."

I stage-whispered to Omid, "Omid, say, 'Hi, what are you working on?'" He did, and I replied abruptly, turning my response into a caricature, "My teddy bear birthday party."

Oftentimes when we struggle in writing conferences, the problem is that we haven't explicitly told kids what their jobs are. We need to come right out and tell children whatever it is we expect them to do.

It is helpful for writers to anticipate that we begin conferences by observing them as they work and that, at some point, we'll want them to teach us what they are working on in their writing.

Notice again that before I demonstrate, I set children up to listen by telling them what I hope they notice. Then I demonstrate by role-playing, not by talking about or summarizing the activity.

Then I said to the kids, "You often do this. You just tell the *topic* of your writing. Here's the sort of answer I *wish* you'd give." I stage-whispered again to Omid, "Omid, ask me again."

Omid again asked, "Hi, what are you working on?"

Again I role-played being a child. "I'm writing about my teddy bear birthday." (Here, in an aside, I name what I just did: "I told the topic I'm writing about.") "And I am trying to write just the important details about the teddy bear birthday—not all the boring details, only the *important* details." (In another aside I say, "That's the work I am doing as a writer.") "I am crossing out the boring parts."

Active Engagement

Ask the children to tell each other the difference between what they often do and what you hope they'll do.

"So, writers, could you tell your partner why it's better to say my topic *and* to say 'I am trying to write the important details about the teddy bear birthday—not just the boring details'?" I listened in as the partners talked to each other.

"I'm hearing you say that at the start of a conference, when I ask, 'What are you working on?' your job is not only to say the topic—the teddy bear birthday—but also to say *what you are trying to do as a writer*. It was good when I said I was trying to take out the boring parts that weren't the important parts of my story."

"So right now, in your mind, could you get ready for a writing conference? Pretend I was just now pulling my chair close to yours and that in a minute, I will ask, 'What are you working on as a writer?' Think about what you will answer when I ask, 'What are you working on as a writer?' Get an answer ready in your mind."

"What are you working on as a writer? Thumbs up when you have an answer.

"So let's try it. 'John, what are you working on as a writer?'"

"I'm revising?"

When I demonstrate something to children, I try to be absolutely blatant with what I'm trying to show. I am not subtle.

Instead of taking the time to call on a few children, I sum up what I've heard. I pretend I'm rearticulating what I heard the children say, but the truth is the children probably haven't said what I hoped they'd say, so I just pretend they did.

Don't dismiss times like this when active involvement means giving children a two-minute silence in which you ask them all to do a particular kind of mental work. In this interval, many children will turn their minds toward practicing what you've discussed.

"What do you think, class? Has John done his job in this conference? I don't think you have quite yet. John, can you tell us *exactly* what you are doing as a writer? Use our chart to help. Are you making a movie in your mind? Adding dialogue? Or what?"

"I'm adding details?"

"Oh! Details about what?"

"About my brother being mad."

"Oh! Now I understand what you are working on. You are trying to add details to show that your brother was mad. Thanks, John."

"Let me ask you each again the question, 'What are you working on as a writer today?' Use this chart to help you think of an answer. Partner two, tell partner one what you are working on as a writer today. Be specific, like John was when he said he's adding details to show his brother was mad. Partner one, tell partner two what you are working on as a writer today."

Link

Remind the children that in conferences with you or with anyone, they need to name the work they are trying to do as writers.

"Today, and for the next few days before I confer with you, I'll tell you ahead of time that I'm coming. I'll give you some time to reread and to think. By the time we start our conference, I want you to be ready to tell me exactly what you are doing as a writer—because that's your job in a conference."

I'd like to add, "And tell it to us—don't ask us," but I keep this comment to myself.

Again John responds as if he's asking a question, as if he were guessing the right answer. I ignore this and respond with certainty.

We need to teach children how to articulate their plans as writers. Often we'll pump them for fragments of information, and then we put these together, as I did here. I could also say, "So, put what you've said together, John, and tell me your plans as a writer."

TIME TO CONFER

Remember to insist that writers name what they are trying to do. Then, typically you'll say, "Show me where you did that." You'll then decide whether you want to teach the child more ways to do what he or she is trying to do, or whether you'll want to suggest an additional goal. See the conferences cited at right.

If children don't seem to have words to describe their intentions, you can give them those words. "Oh! So I see you are adding dialogue, adding talk," you'll say. Or, "Are you trying to give me a more detailed picture of what happened? Smart work!"

Once the writer has told you about her plans for writing, name what the child has done that you hope she will continue to do in the future. To do this, you'll need to extrapolate something generalizable that the child has done.

Review the revision conferences to notice the sort of things we see and support. Heather added a phrase saying where she went bowling and we congratulated her for showing the setting, George writes how time dragged on and we celebrated the way he showed the ticking clock instead of telling. Learn to name what the child has done in one piece in ways that are generalizable across other pieces, because this move occurs not only early in conferences, but also at the end of them—as well as in teaching share sessions.

These conferences in *The Conferring Handbook* may be especially helpful today:

▶ *"This Part Is Confusing to Me"*

▶ *"Can You Reenact That Part in a Way That Shows Me How You Felt?"*

Also, if you have *Conferring with Primary Writers*, you may want to refer to the following conference:

▶ "As a Reader, I'd Love to Hear More About That"

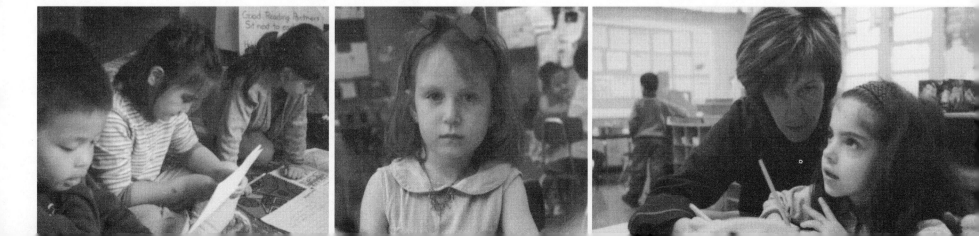

Give the children a chance to practice their roles in conferences.

"Earlier today I told you that you need to be able to tell *me* what you are working on as a writer. You also need to be able to tell *your partner* what you are working on. So partner one, will you say to partner two, 'What are you working on as a writer?' and then listen to what the writer is working on. Use your fingers to collect the things the writer is doing with his or her piece."

The room erupted with talk. Mikey and Joshua talked to each other.

Josh: "So what have you been working on as a writer today?"

Mikey: "I've been trying to revise with details. So far I have 'I went outside.'"

Josh: "Hmm. Mikey, that's not many details. You need to describe *how* you went out."

Mikey: "Oh, yeah. That's right. What do you think I should say?"

Josh: "Say you zoomed out like an arrow."

Mikey: "Okay."

"Convening the class, I said, "Writers, today I listened in on Josh and Mikey. Mikey told Josh he was trying to revise with details, and Josh was able to help him do that. That's the great thing about telling your partner what you're trying to do as a writer. People can help you do what you are often trying to do."

Share sessions often have a teaching point and act almost as minor minilessons. It takes a bit of practice to learn how to teach a series of lessons that together lift children's work up, up, and up.

To be quick and clear, I summarize Josh and Mikey's interaction for the class rather than have them reenact it. I don't go into the details of their work; instead, I pull out the main points.

- Reenact a conference in front of the whole class. For example, "Katya and I were having a conference. I asked her what she was working on as a writer. Katya told me she was writing the story of a dizzy pigeon she saw recently. But she forgot to say what her writing work was. Then she remembered that she has a job to do in a conference. Katya, let's show the class how the conference went after you remembered your job, okay?" Because Katya was prepared to model this conference, she answered, "Well, I am trying to add more details about how the pigeon was moving around in circles in the park. I am revising by adding more words to my piece."

- Summarize a conference: "Yesterday when I was conferring with Colin he did something so smart! When I asked him how it was going, he said. . . ."

- Act as the student and ask the entire class of children together to be the teacher. Have them collectively ask you how it's going. You, then, respond with a content-based answer. "Oh, I am writing about my friend Jonah's new baby!" Exaggerate your "mistake" so that the difference between what you are teaching them to do and what you are teaching them not to do becomes both clearer and more memorable. When they call out, "No, you aren't saying about your writing work!" act dumfounded. "But what do you mean? I am talking about my piece, aren't I?" For active engagement, ask children to turn and talk to each other about how you should have answered the question. Have a couple of partnerships share their suggestions. Someone will say that you need to name what you are working on as a writer instead of simply telling the content of the story.

SHOWING, NOT TELLING

GETTING READY

▶ Child willing to act out an emotion
▶ Piece of writing (a child's or your own), written on chart paper, in which the author explicitly names a feeling he or she had ("I was sad," "I was happy")
▶ Chart paper, marker
● See CD-ROM for resources

BEGIN THIS MINILESSON BY REMINDING WRITERS *that earlier they learned that writers revise by using tools (like carats or inserted paper) toward intentions. It's all too easy for children to fall for the tools alone, and to add, cross out, insert, make flaps, and write new drafts simply because this is a unit on revision and revisions are prized. Once, I saw a child write, stop to scrunch her paper, then write some more. Again she paused to mess up the page. "See, it's all loved up!" she said. We want children to realize that revisions are a means toward a goal, and the goal is better writing.*

This minilesson introduces one of the most basic and essential goals of all dramatic writing: Show, don't tell. If an author says, "I was happy," that is telling. If an author writes, "I skipped all the way home, humming glad songs as if my heart would burst," that's showing. If the author writes, "The classroom was a mess," that's telling. If the author writes, "Books, papers, and tools were strewn everywhere across the classroom, making the place look rather like a teenager's bedroom," that's showing.

You'll encourage writers to revise toward purposes, and you'll suggest writers often revise in an effort to show, not tell.

THE MINILESSON

Connection

Tell the class that today you are going to teach them a new goal they can work toward as they revise. It's often called "show, not tell."

"Writers, we have been trying different ways to revise our pieces. We know writers can use flaps or add pages to a story or they can cross out parts—writers have strategies for revising. Writers also have *reasons* to revise. We revise to add details so readers can picture just what happened, or to reveal the words people said. We also revise to show how we felt, not just to tell our feelings."

Teaching

Read a piece written by one of your children in which the author has summarized, or told, how he was feeling. Then ask that child to show—to act out—what he did when he had that feeling.

Pat began. "Liam is working on a piece about being sad because his team lost a game. He just wrote, 'We lost. I felt sad.' He *told us* how he felt. Writers, instead, try to use words that *show* the reader how the character felt. So Liam is going to try to find the words to *show, not tell*, that he was sad. To do this, he needs to reread his piece and to make a movie in his mind of exactly what he *did*."

Pat had rewritten Liam's piece on chart paper so the whole class could see it. Liam stood at the front of the room and read his piece. The piece ended with, "We lost. I was sad."

"Now Liam, get that sad feeling in you and show us what you did. If we'd been watching, how would we have known you were sad? Show us how you acted when you were sad."

Liam walked slowly, dragging his feet, his head down, his hands stuffed into his pockets.

It is important for children to learn strategies and goals for revision. You may create two separate charts:

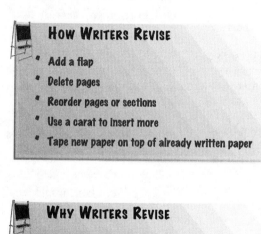

HOW WRITERS REVISE

- Add a flap
- Delete pages
- Reorder pages or sections
- Use a carat to insert more
- Tape new paper on top of already written paper

WHY WRITERS REVISE

- To create the setting
- To make characters talk
- To explain step by step what happened
- To make the story's lead sound more story-like
- To show, not tell

Ask the class to turn and tell their partners the words they'd use to name exactly what the child did to demonstrate the feeling.

> "Tell your partner the exact thing you see Liam doing that shows that he is sad."

Signal for the class to come back together and ask them to share what they noticed. Jot down what the children say in your notebook.

> "His head is down."
>
> "His hands are in his pockets."
>
> "He walks slowly, kicking his feet."
>
> "That's not kicking his feet, that's *dragging* his feet."

Read the original piece and then read a revised version in which you've included the visual detail the children have suggested.

> "This is Liam's first draft: 'We lost. I was sad.' Now listen to the new, show-not-tell draft."

> We lost. I walked slowly along,
> my head down, my hands in my pockets,
> dragging my feet along the ground.

> "That's what a writer does to show, not tell."

Active Engagement

Ask the children to look through their revision folders and see if they can find places in which they can show a feeling instead of telling about it.

> "Would you take a few minutes and quietly look at your writing? See if any of you can find a place where you could show, not tell, how you were feeling. Thumbs up if you found a place."

Link

Tell the children that they now have another way to revise their pieces.

> "Remember when you go off to revise your work today that you can revise in any of the ways we've talked about. Besides showing, not telling, you can add dialogue or revise your lead or add details—or you can invent something different altogether."

There are lots of ways to teach children the importance of "show, not tell." The power of this minilesson is that Pat doesn't just extol the advantages "showing not telling" (as we might do by reading aloud a passage from a children's book in which the author has shown, not told). Instead she helps the class go through the step-by-step sequence of trying to show, not tell. To recreate an emotional experience on the page, many writers reenvision the experience, just as Pat asks Liam and the class to do.

When you want children to notice the way a particular quality of writing improves a draft, it helps to lay contrasting versions alongside each other. Pat repeats Liam's first version here, just before reading the new and improved version.

Each minilesson adds to a cumulating repertoire. It's nice to remind children of their growing number of options.

TIME TO CONFER

You'll definitely want to confer in support of this minilesson because there are few qualities of good writing that will make a bigger difference to your children's work. Elicit the quality of writing you're after by saying,

▶ "If I'd been hiding behind a tree watching you, what would I have seen exactly?"

▶ "Show me what you mean. Get up and act it out. Oh. So are you saying you . . ."

▶ "You said you were (really proud). What, exactly, did you do? Pretend you are doing it now and show me what you'd do. How did it start?"

Once you have elicited a report of what the child did when he or she felt scared, excited, or anxious (for example) repeat what the child said. "I can picture it!: 'I slammed my bedroom door and ran over to my bed. I just lay there looking up at the ceiling.'" You may also want to elicit what the child was thinking. To help the child to write the spoken text down, ask, "So where will you add that?" or say, "Should we cut this page and add paper to make room?" See the conferences cited at right.

Afterwards, help the writer learn from what you've done together. "Do you see what you've done? In your first draft you told—you wrote, 'I was sad,' and now listen to what you've done, 'My heart felt heavy, I tried not to cry. . . .' Why don't you read on and find another place where you *told*, and this time, do the same thing on your own!"

This conference in *The Conferring Handbook* may be especially helpful today:

▶ *"Can You Reenact That Part in a Way That Shows Me How You Felt?"*

Also, if you have *Conferring with Primary Writers*, you may want to refer to the following conferences:

▶ "Make Sure That You're Adding Those Words for a Reason!"

▶ "Are You Doing Revision Work That Makes Important Changes?"

Ask a child to read aloud her first and her revised writing.

"Writers, I want you to see how Samantha revised her piece to show, not tell. Samantha, would you read your first draft?"

My mom kept talking.
I said, "Come on, Mommy!"
But she didn't answer me.

"Samantha wanted to show how she felt so she added this strip of paper and wrote, 'I stamped my foot.' Wasn't that a smart way to show, not tell? Instead of saying, 'I was mad,' Samantha showed how she felt. 'I stamped my foot,' she wrote. Can't you picture her?"

"Tomorrow some of you might want to try to do what Samantha did and revise your writing to show, not tell."

Revisit the "Writers Revise" class chart and add this new revision strategy to it.

"Let's look at our 'Writers Revise' chart. What could we add now to our list?"

WRITERS REVISE

* We reread and make plans.
* We reread, make a movie in our minds, and add words.
* We add details to our drawings.
* We add missing information.
* We add dialogue.
* We subtract things that don't build our main idea.
* We reread and think, "What parts will be confusing?"
* We show, not tell.

During some of the shares, you'll want to read aloud the work of a child who has done whatever you hoped children would do. When you do this, zoom in on the one aspect you are trying to highlight. Don't read a long piece so that your teaching point is lost.

Remember that you always have the option of asking children to show their partner what they did that day.

- Give children practice at showing, not telling. You may want to tell of a time when you felt an emotion. For example, "When I first walked into the new classroom, I was scared." Remind children that writers try to name exact actions rather than summarizing their feelings, and ask a couple of children to act out what they may have done if they entered the new classroom feeling scared. Meanwhile, recruit the class to help you articulate exactly what the actor was doing.

- Point out how a beloved author uses this strategy. For example, in *Where the Wild Things Are*, when Max is getting ready to sail back home, Maurice Sendak doesn't just write, "The wild things were mad." He writes, "They roared their terrible roars and gnashed their terrible teeth." Children can go on a search for other examples of showing, not telling. This is a search that's sure to yield results.

- Talk about a time in your writing life when you were having trouble showing, not telling. Model how you had to actually get up and move your body to remember more details. Sometimes it is hard for kids to remember that they can do this for themselves, even outside of a conference. Watching you do it helps encourage them. For example, "I was trying to write about when I was waiting for my husband to get back from a long business trip. I wrote, 'I was really excited and nervous,' but then I realized that I was telling, not showing. But I couldn't remember exactly what I did! So I had to actually stand up from my desk at home and pretend that I was there waiting for him so that I could remember what it felt like! When I did that, I remembered that I kept going to the curtain every five seconds to check and see if the taxi was there yet. Every little sound in the hallway I thought might be him. I was so jumpy that when the phone rang, I nearly fell off my chair. My feet kept tapping and I read the same sentence in my book six times in a row!" Point out to children that including those details is a way to show, not tell.

To efficiently study your children's understandings of show, not tell, say, "If you did some show-not-tell revisions, leave a sticky note on the section of your text where you did this and put your writing in my show-not-tell take-home box." When you study what your children think is entailed in showing, not telling, you'll probably notice:

▸ Many children try to show, not tell, and some of their efforts add tremendously to their stories. This is a concept that can really pay off.

▸ Some children misunderstand. They may add descriptive words, thinking that the word *show* means *add adjectives*. If the child wrote, "The cute, frisky dog looked at me," this is still *telling* because the writer has *told* that the dog is cute and frisky. The writer could, instead, *show* that the dog is cute and frisky by writing, "The dog caught a leaf, and turned a somersault. Then it spun around in a circle."

▸ Some children's revisions lead to show *and* tell (rather than show, *not* tell) writing. Such a child might write: "I felt sad. I had tears on my face," which is telling and then showing. These children can be taught that showing, alone, is enough.

▸ Some children will understand *showing* when they are showing feelings more easily than other forms of showing. They'll show how a character acted when he or she was angry, confused, or happy much more quickly than they'll show that a morning was frantic or a bedroom was messy.

▸ When students take a word (sad) and revise it to make it into a showing phrase or sentence, they may not reread to make sure their sentences are still coherent.

LEARNING MORE ABOUT SHOWING, NOT TELLING

GETTING READY

▶ Story you've been revising throughout this unit
▶ Revision marker
▶ *Mike Mulligan*, by Virginia Lee Burton, or another book in which the author has shown, not told
● See CD-ROM for resources

SOME CONCEPTS REQUIRE—AND DESERVE—MORE ATTENTION *than others. You'll want to spend a few days emphasizing that writers show rather than tell.*

One way to linger on a concept is to teach the same content differently. In Session VIII, you used a child's writing to illustrate the value of showing, not telling. In this session, you'll find your example in children's literature.

This minilesson also raises the ante and teaches a more complex form of showing, not telling. Your point will be that writers show, not tell, not only when bringing feelings to life, but also when describing almost anything. For example, instead of saying, "It was crowded when the relatives visited," in her book The Relatives Came, *Cynthia Rylant writes:*

> The relatives weren't particular about beds, which was good since there weren't any extras, so a few squeezed in with us and the rest slept on the floor, some with their arms thrown over the closest person, or some with an arm across one person and a leg across another.

In this session, you'll use well-known and well-loved books to teach the class how to show, not tell.

The Minilesson

Connection

Tell your students they are doing a great job of showing, not telling, how they *feel* in their writing. Tell them that today you are going to teach them that they can show, not tell, all the time, not just when they write about feelings.

"Writers, I brought your writing with me to a coffee shop yesterday, and I was sitting there drinking my coffee and reading your pieces. I couldn't believe how amazing your revisions were—they added so much! I wanted to go up to people at the coffee shop and say, 'Excuse me—may I show you the changes Patrick made when he revised to show, not tell?' But I held in my excitement. You did a great job of showing, not telling, how you felt."

"Today I want to teach you that writers use this advice all the time, not just when we write about feelings. Writers also *show* the darkness of a gray sky, the length of a trip. They show that a dog's bark was startling. In fact, writers can use 'show, not tell' as a rule for most writing."

Teaching

Tell a vignette about a time you were told that showing, not telling, is one of the biggest rules of all.

"Let me tell you a story. Several summers ago, I heard that a writer I love was signing books at the bookstore. I didn't have any money to buy one of her books, but I wanted to talk with her, so I waited in a big long line and finally I reached her. She expected me to have one of her books and to ask for her signature, but I didn't have any. So we just looked at each other. And I said, 'I love your writing. What is your secret?' And she said, 'Lucy, I have three words to tell you. Just three. But they are the secret to really good writing.' Then she looked me in the eyes and said, 'Show, not tell.'"

"Years later, I still have those words pinned on the bulletin board over my desk."

I begin this minilesson by telling the story of how I read the children's writing at the coffee shop because I want to show (not tell) the children that I think about them when they're not near me. I'm hoping to create a sense that I've been saving up things to tell them and now need their full attention.

The teaching method I use in this minilesson is that I explain and give an example. The challenge when using this method is to say something memorable. It is easier to make an impression when we demonstrate than when we explain.

Give an example of a beloved author who follows the advice to show, not tell.

"Virginia Lee Burton took that advice when she wrote *Mike Mulligan*. She *could* have said, 'When the steam engine Mike started digging, there was a lot of noise and dirt.' But she didn't want to just *tell* it—she wanted to *show* it. So she wrote this."

> Dirt was flying everywhere, and the smoke and steam were
> so thick that the people could hardly see anything. But
> listen! "Bing! Bang! Crash! Slam!"

Active Engagement

Get the whole class to help you rewrite part of a draft to show, not tell. Ask your students to imagine the story as a "movie in their minds" and to describe what they envision.

"Let's practice showing, not telling, together by looking back at the story we wrote earlier about the mouse."

> It was a morning meeting.
> Everyone heard a noise coming from the couch.
> "Everyone, listen to the story," Pat said. "Forget that noise, it's nothing."
> Patrick jumped up.
> "I heard it again," he said.
> We saw there was a mouse under the cushion.
> We thought it was a toy mouse. And then Pat started to pick it up but we
> screamed because it was a real mouse!

"Let's try, with a partner, to show and not tell the part where Pat goes to pick up the toy mouse only to find out it is real. Talk to your partner about how you would revise this part to show it. Remember exactly what Pat did, and say what you saw her doing. If you can't remember, make it up."

Almost any story contains examples of show, not tell. Be sure to select a story the class knows well. In Owl Moon, Jane Yolen shows how cold it was. In A Chair for My Mother, Vera B. Williams shows that it was chaotic outside the burning apartment building.

To highlight the concept, make up the alternative as I did when I said, "Burton could have just said, 'There was a lot of noise,' but instead she. . . ."

Notice that this one text threads through a third of the minilesson in this unit.

To make this clear, I direct the class to a specific part of the text to revise rather than have them consider the whole text. I don't want them to spend time deciding what to revise. My aim here is to have them practice the mind work behind showing, not telling.

Solicit your children's recollections of the incident and incorporate these details into the draft.

After a few minutes, I reconvened the class.

"May I interrupt? I heard you saying you want to add this."

Pat started to pick it up but we screamed because it was a real mouse! Pat calmly reached out to pick up the stuffed mouse. She reached her hand toward the stuffed animal and suddenly it bolted off the sofa, across the rug, and into our classroom. We watched in shock.

Link

Ask the children to locate sections in their writing that merit revisions toward the goal of showing, not telling.

"I know you are going to think about showing, not telling, whenever you write. Start today. Open your folders and take a look at the piece you are going to work on today. Find a place where you can show, not tell. Once you have found that place, you may walk to your seat and get started."

MID-WORKSHOP TEACHING POINT

Intervene to tell the class about one child who revised by showing, not telling.

"Writers, may I stop all of you? I want to show you the smart revision work Emma just did. She had written this page of her story." [*Fig. IX-1*]

"She reread her story and said, 'I told them it was yucky but I never really showed what that medicine was like.' So she added a little secret code—see this box? It says, 'go to the next page'—and on another page she tried to show what the medicine was like. She wrote this." [*Fig. IX-2*]

"So Emma has tried to show, not tell. How many of the rest of you are finding big ways to make your writing a lot better? Great. Get back to work then."

If you want to move the minlesson along, just say what you heard rather than eliciting this from young spokespeople.

Although most workshops end with a reminder of all the many possible ways writers might revise, this minilesson makes it very clear that showing, not telling, is more than just one option among many.

Fig. IX-1 Emma
I had to take yucky yucky medicine. (Go to next page) It was so yucky I hated it. I had a fever. I got better after I took it.

Fig. IX-2 Emma
I had to crack and chew them and I thought, "When will I get better?"

TIME TO CONFER

Review the conferences cited at right. The unit of study will soon round its final bend, and so you'll want to be sure, in your conferences, to look across a child's portfolio writing and revision to see what it is that the child can do, what he or she does with automaticity, and what he or she seems on the verge of doing. Ask the child to join you in noticing how his or her writing has changed. Is it more readable? Does it sound more literary? Has the volume of writing the child is able to do increased substantially? By now, you should expect to see dramatic, palpable growth in these and other dimensions. If you have a few children who aren't growing visibly as writers, you probably want to confer with these children every day, and be sure to get them started doing the work you expect while you are still there in a conference.

This conference in *The Conferring Handbook* may be especially helpful today:

▶ *"Can You Reenact That Part in a Way That Shows Me How You Felt?"*

Also, if you have *Conferring with Primary Writers*, you may want to refer to the following conferences:

▶ "Make Sure That You're Adding Those Words for a Reason!"
▶ "Are You Doing Revision Work That Makes Important Changes?"

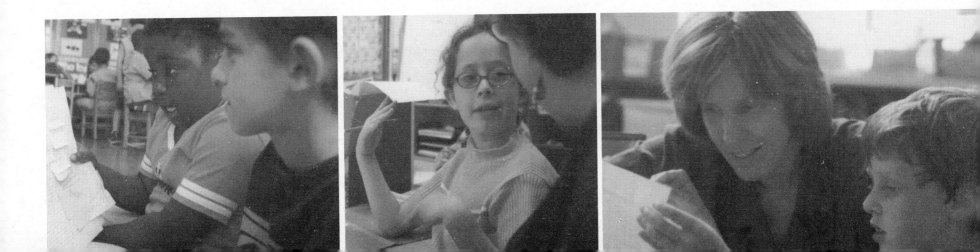

Celebrate the improvements you've seen because writers are revising to show, not tell. Read what one child wrote before and after he revised.

"It's like someone has waved a magic wand over your stories, they are so much better today. Listen to some of the revisions you all made—and notice how the writing gets better! Patrick, will you read your first draft to the class?"

Patrick read, "'When I went to Sea World I was excited.'"

"Okay, now read your next draft, the one that shows, not tells."

Patrick eagerly complied. [*Fig. IX-3*]

"Patrick's second draft is a lot better, isn't it? I can picture the whole thing happening, the way he paints the whole scene. Patrick, you really worked hard as a writer to show, not tell."

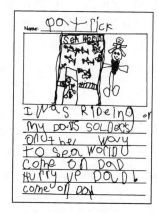

I was riding on my Dad's shoulders on the way to Sea World. "Come on Dad! Hurry Up Dad! Come on."

"We don't want to miss the dolphin show do we? Or the sea creatures show. Do we want Sea World to close?" "Sea World closes at night," Dad said. "Oh," I said. "But let's hurry."

Fig. IX-3   Patrick

If this piece is a bit confusing to you, you're not alone! But Patrick is nevertheless growing as a writer and attempting new and more challenging forms of writing. Growth doesn't necessarily lead to better writing!

Read aloud excerpts from children's writing that deserve to be revised. Ask children to tell each other how they'd revise these passages.

"So today, I'm going to read you a couple of pieces of writing I've seen in your folders, and will you listen for places where you might—if you were the author—revise the piece so you were showing, not telling, like Patrick did?"

"Are you ready to listen? I'll read the story twice, then you tell your partner how you might rewrite it if the story was yours."

It was my turn to bat. I was nervous. I didn't hit the ball. My team was out. I was sad.

The youngsters talked to their partners. Instead of asking them to share their ideas with the class, I went on to read the next excerpt. Again partners discussed how they'd revise it to show not tell.

My sister had a birthday. Everyone gave her presents. She made a mess. Then we had cake.

Remind writers that you've been teaching a concept they can use another day with another piece.

"Writers, tomorrow and for the rest of your life, the important thing will be to see places in your own writing where the piece could be stronger if you showed what was happening rather than just telling it."

This is a great way to give kids a lot of practice. It's wise to give them a pile of excerpts.

Don't feel that you need to elicit the "right" answer or that the partner conversations only count if you have children report back on what they said.

REVISING ENDINGS

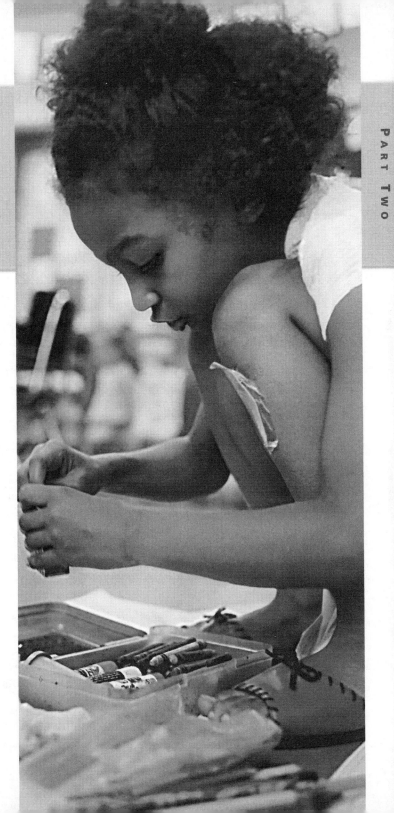

GETTING READY

▶ Two pieces of writing (the children's or your own) in which the endings have been revised (you may want the new ending to resolve a problem)

▶ *Koala Lou*, by Mem Fox, or another book that demonstrates a good ending

⬤ See CD-ROM for resources

EARLIER THIS YEAR, DURING THE SMALL MOMENTS UNIT, *you noticed that many of your children ended their pieces with "and then I went home" or "I went to bed." In a minilesson designed to encourage children to revise their endings, you suggested that effective endings usually don't jump away from the focused event. You told children that sometimes you can simply tell the next thing that happened and that will suffice as a good ending—as when the lady with a snake visited the class and then put the snake back in the crate. Alternatively, you pointed out then, another way to tend a piece is to show how you felt. "The lady locked the crate, and I smiled." At the time, you made a rule: You can't end a piece by saying, "And then I went home."*

Endings are crucial because they are the last thing a reader reads, and therefore they leave a lasting impression. One writer has said that poems and stories are like love affairs—you can forgive anything as long as they have a good ending. (But don't tell this to the children!)

In today's minilesson, you could remind your children of their previous conversation about endings and go a step further to teach children that they can study ways other writers end their pieces. More specifically, you'll show children how you reread and savored the strong ending a child wrote. You'll talk about how the ending works well, but your larger message will be that writers study good writing.

This minilesson, then, will remind children that they can study stories written by other authors to glean ideas for how to write effective endings.

The Minilesson

Connection

Tell the children that whenever you read the ending of a story, your intonation signals that this is the end. Read the last page of _Koala Lou_ as an example.

"Once I took a course with Mem Fox, the author of _Koala Lou_. She taught us to tell and read stories really well. One tip she gave us is that when you come to the end of a story, your voice needs to close . . . down . . . the . . . story. She taught us that when we read the ending of a book or a poem, our voices can make the end feel like the _amen_ at the end of a prayer, or the _goodnight_ at the end of a day, or the _so long_ at the end of a visit."

"Listen as I read the ending of Mem's book, _Koala Lou_. You remember how Koala lost the race and crept home, sad. But then her mother found her. The book ends like this."

> Her mother said, "Koala Lou, I do love you," and she hugged her for a very long time.

Tell the children that as a reader, you know that it is important to let your voice show that an ending is special. Tell the children that you try to _write_ endings that will sound good.

"Because I read endings as if they are the most special words in the world, when I write, I always go back and revise my endings to make them worthy. Today let's think about how to make our endings special."

Teaching

Tell the children you emulate endings in published texts.

"I love to study the work of other authors. I get ideas from what other authors do. When I find an ending I love, I look back on it and think, 'What did that author do that worked so, so well?'"

"So watch me now as I read an ending I love, and then try to name what the author did that I could try."

I'm convinced that if children read their own writing aloud with reverence they'll write pieces that deserve to be read in such a manner. Teaching children to read their endings with a majestic pace will do more than almost anything to improve the qualities of those endings.

Read the final words slowly, really thinking about their meaning. "She hugged her—for a very . . . long . . . time."

"The story I'm going to read is written by an author named Eric. It goes like this." [*Fig. X-1*]

"I'm trying to think what I love about this ending. I think I love it because it's like there was a big problem—Eric was hoping for more time, Pat refuses, Eric pleads, Pat says no one else is asking—and then suddenly there is an answer to the problem! Suddenly, *everyone* is asking for more time. It was the same in *Koala Lou*. Koala Lou was sad from losing her race, and then, everything feels better because her mother hugs her for a very long time."

"So one way to make a good ending is to make things turn out okay at the end. Maybe, like Koala Lou, you lost the race, or you didn't get what you wanted—but maybe someone is there to comfort you, or maybe you learn a big lesson anyway. One writer said, 'If the dog dies, at least there needs to be a puppy left behind.'"

"So one lesson we could learn is that in many stories, there's a problem that gets solved at the end. But the other, bigger lesson I'm trying to teach is that endings matter, and if we admire an ending that works, we can see what the author did to write that good ending."

Active Engagement

Ask children to decide for themselves why a published story's ending works.

"Let's try it. I'm going to read you another wonderful story, a story by Lisa, and when I reach the end, listen to how my voice sounds as I read the end, and then tell your partner what this author did to make such a nice ending." [*Fig. X-2*]

Telling the children that you love to read and study the work of authors—and then turning to the work of an author from the class—is a nice twist! Try to read the child's writing with as much reverence as you brought to Koala Lou.

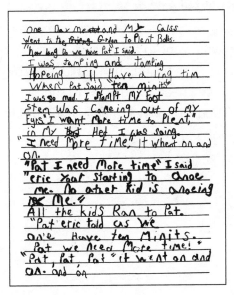

Fig. X-1   Eric

One day me and my class went to the garden to plant bulbs. "How long do we have, Pat?" I said. I was jumping and jumping, hoping I'd have a long time, when Pat said, "Ten minutes." I was so mad. I stomped my foot. Steam was coming out of my ears. "I want more time to plant." In my head I was saying, "I need more time," it went on and on.
"Pat, I need more time," I said.
"Eric, you're starting to annoy me. No other kid is annoying me," [Pat said.]
All the kids ran to Pat, "Pat, Eric told us we only have ten minutes." "Pat, we need more time!" "Pat," "Pat," "Pat," it went on and on and on.

Link

Remind children to take what they learned today to their independent work: remind them to show, not tell, add or subtract, or revise their endings.

"So, writers, you have lots of choices you can make when you think about the work you want to do today as writers. You can reread and think, 'Are there places where I'm telling and I could instead show?' You can think, 'Are there places where I need to add—or to subtract?' And you can practice reading your ending aloud so, so well, then revising the ending so it works even better."

The rule of thumb is that in a good minilesson, we try to make one point. The truth is, however, that sometimes minilessons that make only a single point aren't worth their keep. You'll notice in this minilesson and in many others that I tuck in a few subordinate points. Here, I tuck in a bit of emphasis on reading our endings aloud well. I also mention what I notice when admiring the work of other authors (that the endings resolve the problem). This minilesson wouldn't work as well if I tried to give all these points equal weight.

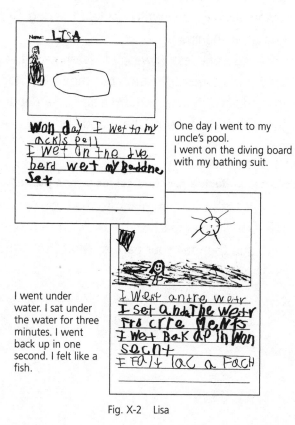

One day I went to my uncle's pool.
I went on the diving board with my bathing suit.

I went under water. I sat under the water for three minutes. I went back up in one second. I felt like a fish.

Fig. X-2   Lisa

TIME TO CONFER

Each day, your minilesson has added a new item to children's repertoire. Be careful that your conferences don't convey the message that each day, you expect children to incorporate the strategy from that particular day's minilesson into their writing. Instead, your conferences need to convey the idea that these children now have a growing repertoire of strategies they can draw upon—including all that you've taught in this unit and in previous units. See the conferences cited at right. Use the conferring checklist to remind you of lessons you've taught, and make a special point to keep these particularly important concepts alive in your room:

▶ Writers reread and think about their writing.

▶ Writers add on to particular sections for a reason. They may add on to bring out dialogue, to show the setting, or to help people know the internal as well as the external story.

▶ Writers know that when a character feels something, it helps to show what the character does that conveys the feeling.

▶ Writers think carefully about their beginnings and endings.

▶ Writers write readable writing, and reread often, making small changes so others will have an easier time reading the text.

These conferences in *The Conferring Handbook* may be especially helpful today:

▶ *"This Part Is Confusing to Me"*

▶ *"Can You Reenact That Part in a Way That Shows Me How You Felt?"*

Also, if you have *Conferring with Primary Writers*, you may want to refer to the conferences in part four.

Ask the children to choose a piece to read aloud well and to pay special attention to how they read the ending. Tell them that as they do this, they may find things they'll want to revise.

"Writers, would you choose one piece from your revision folder that you really, really like and would you do this? Read it aloud to yourself. Read it like it is worth a million dollars. Slow down at the ending. Stretch it out. Then, if you have more time, read your beautiful piece to your partner as well. Sometimes when you do this, you'll find things to change."

If Children Need More Time

- Give four or five familiar books to clusters of four children and ask them to notice different ways authors end books. If you have time to engineer this, give each group a couple of books that end similarly. For example, one group could have two books in which the ending refers back to the beginning and two books in which the problem is solved. Another group could have two books that end with dialogue and two that end with the characters feeling happy again.

- Have the students practice reading their pieces out loud in the same way mentioned in the share. Have them "take care" of the ending—like Mem Fox taught—and end it like a song or a prayer, with special attention in their voices as they read. Ask them if the words of their ending help them read it out loud with reverence. If they don't *feel* the ending when they read it out loud, what could be done to make it more meaningful?

- Because your children have been steeped in stories since the beginning of the year, many of them have developed an innate sense of the way that stories go. Have them read pieces they wrote earlier to each other and ask the question, "Does the ending feel right?" This is a potentially ambiguous question, but it opens a space for children to bring their innate sense of story into the workshop. And because of their sense of story, your children will, in fact, be able to sense that many of their stories do not feel finished.

You are turning in to the home stretch, so it's important to use your rubric to check your and your children's progress. Are you accomplishing what you set out to accomplish? What—and who—needs extra attention? The rubric is meant to direct and galvanize your teaching rather than simply to be a source of guilty feelings at the end of your unit! Use it, and plan some small-group strategy lessons based on remaining concerns you have.

REVISING WHILE WRITING

GETTING READY

▶ Overhead projector or chart paper on which to compose a new piece of writing in front of the class

▶ Marker

⊙ See CD-ROM for resources

SOME OF YOUR CHILDREN MAY CLAIM *that they have revised their four selected pieces and have nothing more to do. Others, meanwhile, will still be revising productively. You may decide, therefore, to let children know that writers don't necessarily write an entire piece, finish it, and only then revise it. Some writers begin new pieces, anticipating that from the start they'll often shift between writing and revising. You'll want to suggest that a few children do this, but you'll need to be careful not to make the prospect of writing new pieces sound too enticing—you don't want to lure writers away from the hard work of improving their best pieces.*

In this session, you'll teach children that they can write new pieces, revising as they go.

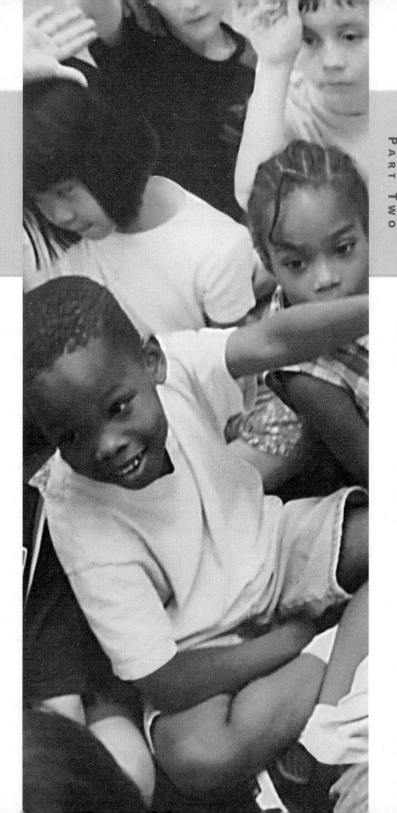

THE MINILESSON

Connection

If your children have revised all their selected pieces, invite them to begin new pieces, planning to revise these before they are complete.

"A few of you came to me yesterday to say, 'We already revised our telling so it would be showing, and we added dialogue, and we tried several leads, and we added details. We took away stuff that didn't go and . . . and . . . and . . . can we be done?'"

"Of course, this is writing time, so we're never done *writing*. But a few of you may want to change from fixing up finished pieces to starting new pieces. And this time, you might write just a page or so before you realize—'Hurrah! I'm *already* getting an idea for how I could revise this!' You won't have to wait till you are done before you start revising! Writers often shift between writing, then revising, then writing, then revising."

Teaching

Use an analogy to show that workers revise *as* they create, not only when the work of creation is done. In this instance, I liken a writer to an artist making a clay rabbit, and show that I shift between making and evaluating.

"Working on our own writing is like working with clay. Have you ever made a clay rabbit? You pull in to work with the clay like this," I leaned in and molded imaginary clay in my hands, "and then, you pull back," I held the imagined clay rabbit at arms length and eyed it, "and you think, 'How do I like it? What can I do to make it even better?' Maybe you think, 'Wait, that ear is crooked.' Pretty soon you are back at work."

"Did you notice that as *I am working*, I am also revising? I *work* with the clay. I *stop and look* at my work, then I *think about* what I like and what I want

Notice the message: as children write first drafts, they'll be thrilled to see possibilities for revision—and to realize that, hurrah, revision needn't be postponed until the end of a piece!

I've used this metaphor for twenty years! Borrow it. You'll probably find, as I do, that it makes the entire minilesson more concrete and that you can refer to it often in later conferences and minilessons.

to improve. Then I *revise* my work with the clay. As writers, we *work* that way too: we work on our writing, we *stop and reread*, we *think about* what we like about it and what we could make better, and then we *revise* our writing."

Compose a new piece of writing on chart paper in front of the class.

"Watch me as I write and revise."

"Okay, so I'm going to write about our work with reading buddies yesterday. Let's see, I'm trying to remember how it started."

> After lunch, we talked about recess. Then we listened to the book *Fudgeamania*. Then at two o'clock, there was a knock on the door. Mica said, "They are here!"

"Wait, let me *stop and reread*. Hmm . . . how do I like this? What could I change? I'm thinking it starts slowly. Maybe I have too much that doesn't really go with reading buddies. I should take away some stuff." I crossed out a few phrases and my new version read:

> After lunch, we listened to *Fudgeamania* until there was a knock on the door. "They're here," Mica called, and our fourth-grade reading buddies came in.

Active Engagement

Ask the children to tell each other what you did to go from writing to revising to writing again. Recruit a few children to tell the class what they said to their partner.

"So what do you think? Turn and tell your partner how I revised my work as I was writing." As always, I gave them a minute or two to talk with their partners while I listened in, then convened the class. "How did I revise my work as I was writing?"

"First you started to write."

"You stopped to reread."

"Then you crossed things out and fixed your story."

Because children experience minilessons as oral rather than written texts, I incorporate the language and literary devices of great speeches into my minilessons. Martin Luther King's "I Have a Dream" speech is worth studying as an exemplar text. In that speech, as in many great speeches, there is a lot of repetition: "I have a dream that one day . . . I have a dream that. . . ." Use repetition and parallel construction in your minilessons.

You may have noticed that the teaching component of this minilesson has two parts. The first half, in which I show how the clay rabbit metaphor pertains to my own writing process, could have been tweaked so that it also provided an exercise text that the class imagined revising. Instead, I write, reread, and revise a story in front of the class, showing them my blow-by-blow process. Because this makes the teaching component of the minilesson long and complex, the upcoming active engagement section is short and simple.

Don't call on more than three children!

Link

Highlight the fact that you shifted between composing and revising. Tell the children they may decide to do the same during workshop time.

"You noticed I didn't finish writing the whole reading-buddies story before I started to revise. As writers, we can write a bit, then stop and say, 'What's good that I can build on?', 'What's not so good that I can fix?' then we can go back to work."

"If any of you feel as if all four of your selected pieces are totally revised, you can begin a new piece. This time, please shift between pulling in to write, and pulling back to reread and to question. Okay. Off you go."

As I explain this, I use the same gestures I did when telling the clay rabbit story during the teaching part of the minilesson. I pull in as if I am writing, then I hold my imaginary piece away to look at it, and then I pull in again as if I am ready to revise. I use the analogy of the artist making a clay rabbit throughout the lesson.

MID-WORKSHOP TEACHING POINT

Remind children to use the writing conventions they know as best they can.

"Writers, this morning I noticed Aziz rereading his piece, pointing under each word. I asked him what he was doing and he said, 'I'm making sure I spelled my words as right as I can.' It is really smart to pause in the midst of writing to do that. Today, right now, would you each take a minute to use Aziz's strategy of rereading very slowly and carefully, checking every word? Make sure you spelled your words as best you can. Do that now."

Alternatively, you can ask children to check that they are writing with punctuation, using lowercase letters (unless they're at the start of a sentence or the beginning of someone's name), or doing some other type of work on conventions that you want them to keep in mind as they write.

TIME TO CONFER

You'll probably find that your children leap at the chance to write some brand new stories. You'll want to confer early, when the stories are being planned or begun. If a story lacks focus, there's no reason to wait until the text is fully written before deciding to zoom in on just one part of it. And if a writer takes time at the start of his or her writing process to revise the lead, the deliberately crafted lead can lift the level of the entire piece. There are lots of reasons, therefore, to encourage children to pause often as they write, to reread and rethink. On the other hand, this can lead a few children into a cycle of endless futile revisions; to confer well, you have to know your children and know their needs. See the conferences cited at right from the *Conferring with Primary Writers* book.

These conferences in *The Conferring Handbook* may be especially helpful today:

▶ *"This Part Is Confusing to Me"*

▶ *"Can You Reenact That Part in a Way That Shows Me How You Felt?"*

▶ *"Study an Example to Get Ideas for Revision"*

Also, if you have *Conferring with Primary Writers*, you may want to refer to the following conferences:

▶ "As a Reader, I'd Love to Hear More About That"

▶ "What Is The Most Important Part of Your Story?"

Ask the children to work with their reading partners to make today's writing as readable as possible.

"Writers, earlier today you paused to check on your spelling. The real trick is to make sure other people can read your writing, right? So today, would you go to your reading partner (not your writing partner) and check whether *your reading partner* has any trouble reading your pieces? If he or she does have trouble, work together to fix things. You might need to use the word wall to help with words, you might need to listen for some sounds, you might need to check your punctuation. If you have time, you can go to other pieces you've revised."

These books can give you a feel for the importance of shifting between a focus on process, on qualities of good writing, on expectations for the workshop, and on convention, but you'll want to decide when to use your share as a time to spotlight conventions. It needn't be today.

You may want to ask children who began a new piece today to put those pieces in a special tray so you can study what they've done. You want to notice two things. First, notice whether these children seem to have cycled between drafting and revising. Is there any evidence that they paused in the act of writing, reconsidered what they were writing, and tried again? If you see evidence of this, rejoice, because it suggests that some of your children are writing with a new attentiveness, a new deliberateness to craft. Also notice whether you see evidence that children who earlier revised to bring a quality of good writing to their work now internalize those qualities, incorporating them into their first drafts. If a child fixed up three old leads, you will want to notice whether now, as she approaches the challenge of writing a brand new lead, she incorporates what she learned from trial and error into her new work. If you see any evidence of this, be sure to point this out to the writer.

PARTNERING FOR REVISION

GETTING READY

▸ Two "Conferring Center" signs posted in the room
▸ Children's current writing brought to the minilesson
◉ See CD-ROM for resources

YOUR CHILDREN HAVE GOTTEN EXCITED ABOUT REVISION, *and a lot of them are doing wonderful work. This emphasis on revision will no doubt also create a hunger in them for conferences with you, and consequently you may find six kids in a line behind you hoping for direction! When this happens, it's time to teach children to rely more on each other.*

This session will teach that "There isn't just one teacher, but twenty-eight teachers in this class! You all must become writing teachers for each other."

The Minilesson

Connection

Tell the class that at one point during the last session, you found a long line of kids behind you needing help. Tell them that you'll teach each of them to be a writing teacher.

"Writers, yesterday I was working with Shariff and I looked up and saw a line of kids that snaked around the room. Everyone in that line was waiting for help from me. So today I want to teach you that there's not just one writing teacher in this class—there are twenty-eight of you!"

"Starting today, there will be two conferring centers set up in the room. See the signs I've put up? If you get stuck, see if there is any free space at a conferring center, and if there is, get a writing teacher to go there with you. Do you know who the writing teachers are? Each and every one of you! Today, I'm going to teach you how to be good writing *teachers*."

Teaching

Demonstrate how children can be writing teachers for one another. First, teach them to read the other's writing.

"So let's say I came to all of you with my story and I said, 'Will you be my writing teacher?' The first thing you need to do is to understand what I'm trying to do. One way to do that is to ask if you can read my writing."

"Can we?"

"Say the whole thing—and act interested, okay? Act like you are dying to read my story. Camilla, you try being my writing teacher and ask if you all can read what I've written."

"Lucy, I see you are holding something. Is that your story? Can we read it?"

"Sure!" I said. I opened my story, written on chart paper, and put it on the easel.

This "oldie but goodie" minilesson has been one of my mainstays for a couple of decades! Don't bypass this one, and don't underestimate its power.

Notice that when I want the class to understand that too many of them are too reliant on me, I zoom in and tell about a very specific episode. "I was working with Shariff and I looked up. . . ." The fact that focus and emblematic detail are qualities of good writing changes not only what I teach, but also how I teach.

I don't explain about the conferring centers while I'm teaching. I try not to let the teaching component of a minilesson be overrun with explanations and assignments. I want instead to reserve that as a time for demonstration. Usually, during the teaching component of a minilesson I'll actually do the thing (or set someone else up to do the thing) that I'm teaching.

When I ask Camilla to "say the whole thing," I'm bringing a strategy I use a lot with English language learners into my minilesson.

On Saturday I went sledding. We drove there. We had two sleds. We had hot chocolate. We went down the hill four times. One time was very icy. Then I went another time. Then we came home.

Shifting gears, I said, "Everyone, I know this isn't the greatest story. Do you think a really good writing teacher says, 'This is boring.'?"

"No!"

Solicit opinions about how to react helpfully to writing, as a writing teacher.

"What do Pat and I do when you have a story like this one? I'm going to give you a few moments to think about this. Thumbs up if you have an idea." I gave them a minute to think about it.

"I bet you are thinking that we ask you to tell us the main thing in your story and we get you to say more about that. Right now, try that. Ask me to tell you the most important thing in my story." Shariff raised his hand as if he were volunteering to ask me the most important part of my story. "Shariff?"

"I think the important part is two sleds."

"Shariff, you are right that I could say that having two sleds was important, but *I'm* the author so I get to be the boss of my piece. I *could* say, 'The most important part was the hot chocolate!' So, Shariff, you need to *ask me*. Ask, 'Lucy, what is the main thing you want to say?' Say that."

"What's the main thing you want to say?"

"Oh! Thanks for asking! What's the main thing I want to say? What a great question. Umm . . . I think I really want to tell about that icy trip because it was really scary."

Offer children some more questions and prompts they might offer one another—and themselves.

Shifting out of the role of writer again, I stage-whispered to one child the next thing I wanted them to ask: "Ask me to tell you all about the icy trip."

"Tell us about it."

I am conscious of shifting roles. Sometimes I'm the writer and sometimes I leave that role and become the teacher coaching the class on how to be good teachers.

I speak as if I know what they were thinking about.

I quickly redirected Shariff's comment. Don't hesitate to put words into your children's mouths. Teach the class the language to use.

Notice how I repeat the child's question. I'm trying to teach children to ask each other, "What's the main thing you want to say?" because in the end, a writer profits from asking that question to himself or herself. The conversations in the classroom between children become conversations a writer has in his or her own mind. This is hugely important work.

I don't solicit the possibilities by saying, "What might you ask me next?" Instead, I provide the words.

"I said to myself, 'I'm going to try the steep hill.' I had butterflies in my stomach. Soon I was on the edge of a cliff. I almost said, 'That's *too* steep,' but I pushed off, and the ground was sheer ice, and I was going and going and. . . ."

Here, I again shifted out of the role of writer and stage-whispered to a child the next thing I wanted him to say: "Interrupt to tell me I should write about this. Tell me to put this in my story."

"You should tell that!"

"Oh! You think so! You think I should put that on my paper? Should I start over and tell it all, step by step, like I've been telling you?"

"Yes!"

"What great writing teachers you've been!"

Active Engagement

Compile a chart to remind children of what to do when they are helping each other write.

"We have a chart called 'Writers Revise,' but I'm thinking we also need to list how to be good writing teachers. We could put the chart over by our conferring centers. Could you and your partner list across your fingers three things writing teachers need to do so we can put them on our chart?"

"I heard you say so many smart things." I repeated some of the things I heard them say and added a couple of things that I pretended they said.

A Writing Teacher's Job

* Writing teachers first read the writer's piece.
* Writing teachers often ask, "What's the main thing you are writing about?"
* Writing teachers get the writer to say more about the main thing.
* Writing teachers say, "You should add that!"

Link

Remind children to go to one another at the Conference Centers today, and from now on.

"Today, and for the rest of your life, if any of you need help, instead of lining up behind me, would you go to the other writing teachers in this classroom?"

Notice that I tell the episode in a blow-by-blow way. I am not summarizing, "It was scary when I went sledding. I had butterflies. I almost fell off." I am, instead, trying to recreate the drama of the moment. The story begins with a small action, as many do.

When I ask children to list across their fingers, I'm using their fingers as graphic organizers for a non-narrative text.

Later, I put these into a chart. I don't want to take the time to write it during the lesson.

It's unlikely that your children will have created such a nice list, but don't let that stop you.

Time to Confer

Today's minilesson reminded children that they can go to each other for help—so now's your chance to confer less and watch more. Use the conferring checklist to help you see what your children are doing with independence. As you watch, you'll see that lots of your children are almost, but not quite, doing something. This will nudge you to switch from watching into conferring—and to confer with a light touch. You can start these conferences by telling children what you saw them doing, by highlighting the wisdom of their actions, and then by saying, "May I make one suggestion?" Your conferences, then, will not be too different from a minilesson.

Of course, if you see a cluster of children who could benefit from similar instruction, pull that group together for a strategy lesson. Again, name what they are doing, suggest what they could do next, and ask them to get started while you watch and offer some guided practice. See "Focus: A Strategy Lesson" and "A Strategy Lesson for Some Proficient First Grade Writers" from the *Conferring with Primary Writers* book.

These conferences in *The Conferring Handbook* may be especially helpful today:

▶ *"This Part Is Confusing to Me"*
▶ *"Can You Reenact That Part in a Way That Shows Me How You Felt?"*
▶ *"Study an Example to Get Ideas for Revision"*

Also, if you have *Conferring with Primary Writers*, you may want to refer to the following conferences:

▶ Focus: A Strategy Lesson
▶ A Strategy Lesson for Some Proficient First Grade Writers

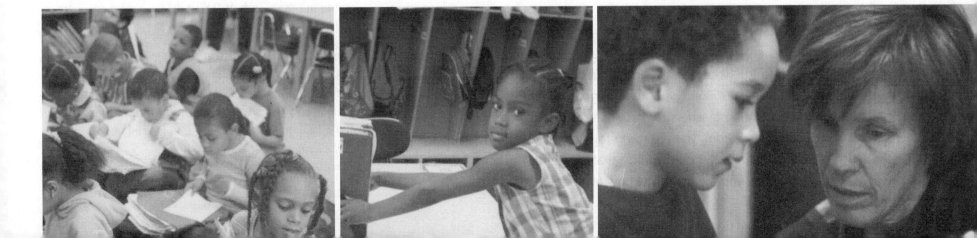

AFTER-THE-WORKSHOP SHARE

Review with the children what a writing teacher needs to do.

"I've seen some wonderful writing teachers so far today. You are going to take over my job soon! Romi needs some help with her writing, so let's practice by being writing teachers for her. Let's reread the chart to remember."

Together with the whole class, be a writing teacher for one child.

"Okay, who could start us off being Romi's teacher? Heather?"

"Can we see your story?"

Romi held the paper up so everyone could see it.

"Class, is that working? What do you need to ask her to do?"

"Will you read it?"

> Last night my mom read to me. Brian kept playing around. We said, "Stop." He stopped. Then she read some more. Brian liked the story and I liked the story and Mom liked the story. It was funny.

"Let's see, what's next, writing teachers?" I gestured to the chart so the class would use it to guide the work. "George?"

"What's it mainly about? How your mom read the story?"

"And Brian was being a pain," Romi added.

Again, I gestured to the next item on the chart, and enlisted Eric to read it and ask Romi the question: "Say more."

"That's all. That's what happened, really."

"Writing teachers, this is the hardest part of your job. You have to get really good at getting the writer to say a lot about the story. I'll give you some hints and we'll practice—but Romi, you need to go out in the hall so we can practice being good writing teachers for you, okay? Close the door. Thanks."

"You need to show Romi you are *dying* to know all about how reading time with her mom went. How could you do that? Pretend I'm Romi. Ask in a way that makes me feel you are dying to know all about reading time."

A WRITING TEACHER'S JOB

* Writing teachers first read the writer's piece.
* Writing teachers often ask, "What's the main thing you are writing about?"
* Writing teachers get the writer to say more about the main thing.
* Writing teachers say, "You should add that!"

It is important that the charts in your classroom are written so all your children can read them. If you are teaching kindergarten children, you may want to alter a chart such as this one so that it includes fewer words. It's wise, however, to include many high-frequency words. For example, instead of listing key words only (reread, question, listen, prompt) you may write:

▶ *I can read my friend's writing.*
▶ *I can ask my friend a question.*
▶ *I can listen to my friend.*
▶ *I can say "Add it!" to my friend.*

You will also want to include simple, iconographic pictures next to each bulleted item to remind children what the words mean.

I help the lesson move along by keeping the class focused on the chart we just created. This lets us avoid getting into content questions, such as, "What did your mom read?" or "What was the funny part?"

Don't hesitate to send the writer into the hall so that you can prep the rest of the class on ways to be good teachers. The hoopla brings added importance to the advice you are going to give kids and makes them listen more keenly. It's also a lot of fun! It helps if you lean forward and whisper as if sharing a secret.

"What'd you do?"

"My mom read." I used a curt voice, making clear I wasn't going to say more.

Then I shift gears. "Okay, let's work together. Let me know you care! I'll be Romi and reread my story again and this time, get me wanting to tell you more."

> Last night my mom read to me. Brian kept playing around. We said, "Stop." He stopped. Then she read some more. Brian liked the story and I liked the story and Mom liked the story. It was funny.

I role-play a tough conference so that they have to try other things.

"Was it was annoying when Brian was playing around?"

Role-playing Romi, I said, "Yeah! 'Cause he was banging on a drum and I couldn't hear. He kept circling me and Mom."

Once again I returned to being the teacher. "See how you got me to talk, nice job! Let's get Romi back in and try it with her piece. Romi, let's start the whole teaching time over again."

"Can we see your story?"

"Should I read it?" Romi asked, and proceeded to do so.

"It must have made you mad at Brian."

"Yeah, 'cause we couldn't concentrate and my mom said, 'Ignore him, he's a baby.' But he was climbing on my leg and spitting."I pointed to the chart again to reminded the class to check it.

Anna said, "You should add that in your story!"

Ask the children to act as writing teachers with their partners.

"Nice suggestion, Anna. Would all of you get with your partners and for today, partner one will be the writer and partner two will be the writing teacher. Do this slowly, and we'll spend the whole share session time just on partner one's story. I'm going to admire what you writing teachers do." I listened and coached their writing teacher work, not their writing work.

Your goal is to teach writing teachers to really be interested in the writer's story and to either use active listening (in which they repeat what the writer said) or prompts ("Tell me all about it!") or open-ended questions ("What happened exactly?") to elicit more.

Don't hesitate to put words in children's mouths today. Whisper to the writing teacher, "Ask her 'why?'" or "Show her you are interested."

There is no question that this minilesson requires and deserves follow-up. You don't need to vary the procedures a great deal. Another day, you can recruit the class to be writing teachers for yet another child. Send this writer into the hall just as I did with Romi, and then you can again assume the role of the writer for a few minutes and again have the class practice with you. Plan on making these points when the occasion presents itself.

- Encourage children to ask questions that get the writer to say a lot, rather than questions that yield one-word answers. I do this by giving very curt, brief answers to questions such as "Is your dog cute?" If the child rewords this to be, "Tell us what your dog looks like," I reward the speaker with a detailed response.

- Encourage children to speak up if they are confused. If a writer says, "We had fun because of stuff," be publicly, dramatically confused. Help children realize that when they are confused, they need to say so to the writer. It helps to provide them with the words, too. They might say, "I'm confused. Will you explain it again?"

REVISING ONE'S GENRE

GETTING READY

- Revision folders brought to the meeting area
- Writing paper cut in half lengthwise
- Paper formatted to look like a letter (line for the date, line for the salutation, lines for the body of the letter, a line for the closing, and a line for the signature)
- How-to paper (turn paper horizontally, make three frames with lines for writing under each frame)
- Chart paper cut in half lengthwise
- Chart paper formatted with lines to look like a letter (see above)
- Chart How-to paper (see above)
- Marker
- "Writers Revise" chart
- See CD-ROM for resources

ONE SURE-FIRE WAY TO IGNITE NEW ENERGY *for revision is to let children know that writers sometimes revise by looking at their material and thinking, "What else could I make of this?"*

Teachers often worry about issuing a wide-open invitation to rewrite narratives to make poems, procedural texts, fictional stories, and the like. Just because you haven't taught a genre doesn't mean children have no sense of it. You'll be amazed at how much children have picked up about many of these genres just from living shoulder-to-shoulder with them. Children learn about genres from each other and from texts they admire. If you have examples in the classroom, they can go to these to get the gist of what a genre might be like.

Above all, ask yourself, what's the worst thing that could happen? What harm will be done if, for a week, children write less-than-great poems or awful stories? At the very least, they'll learn that the content of a piece can be refashioned into a variety of genres, and you'll learn what they know about other genres. At most, they'll tap into a whole new energy source for writing and for revision. They'll learn how to learn.

So trust us. Give this a go, unroll the idea with enthusiasm and confidence (even if you must pretend to be confident), and I can almost promise you'll be delighted in the end.

In this session, you'll teach toward the general point that sometimes a writer revises by looking at a text and thinking, "I could reshape this into a different genre."

Connection

Tell the children that writers sometimes revise by thinking, "I could reshape this."

"Writers, today I have big and important news for you. Listen. This is my news. When writers revise, sometimes we look at what we've made and we think, 'I could shape this differently—and turn it into a poem, or a letter, or a magazine article, or a song—or anything!'"

Teaching

Suggest to the class that they could reread the class story and imagine it in a different genre. Solicit ideas for other genres they could write, and hear how each would start.

"I know Ms. Chiarella teaches this to her fourth graders. This may be too grownup of an idea for you first graders, but let's see if you can understand what I'm saying."

"What I'm saying is that we *could* stand back from our mouse story and we *could* think, 'Hmm. I think I could make something new out of that . . . and I think it should be . . . (and then we decide).' If we did make something new, we'd need to write it on a different kind of paper, so let me show you what we've got. I have poetry paper and newspaper article paper and How-to book paper and letter paper." As I mentioned each, I held it up. "Let's try it. I'll read the mouse story, and then will you and your partner see if you can imagine this as a different kind of thing—a poem, or a letter, or an article for the newspaper, or something else?"

> It was morning meeting.
> Everyone heard a noise coming from the couch.
> "Everyone, listen to the story," Pat said. "Forget that noise, it's nothing."
> Patrick jumped up.
> "I heard it again," he said.
> We saw there was a mouse under the cushion.

At the start of a minilesson, you want your children's full attention. You may want to reread the beginning of thirty minilessons to collect various ways a teacher might start a minilesson. This one is a nice alternative and could set up almost any minilesson.

Whenever possible in a minilesson, it helps to have something concrete to hold, to show. But in this minilesson, it is especially important. The different kinds of paper make the different options vastly more concrete and help children grasp the general concept that a text that's been written one way can be written in different ways.

We thought it was a toy mouse. And then Pat started to pick it up but we screamed because it was a real mouse!
Pat calmly reached out to pick up the stuffed mouse. She reached her hand toward the stuffed animal and suddenly it bolted off the sofa, across the rug, and into our classroom. We watched in shock.

"I know this is *really hard* but try thinking if this could be a poem." I hold up poetry paper. "Or a letter?" I hold up stationery. "Turn and talk!"

After a bit, I asked, "Can *any* of you think of how we could write this differently? Sasha?"

"Me and Shariff thought it could be a poem."

"How might you start it if this was a poem?"

"We were thinking, 'It's not a louse but a mouse?'"

"So you were going to write a rhyming poem? That's one option, isn't it? Did any of you think of making it into a non-rhyming poem, one with exactly true words like the words in the Langston Hughes poem we read in the mornings?"

"We did. We thought it could go, 'The room was as silent as the night then a squeak and a scream and. . . .'"

List suggested options on the chart.

"So we have two great options. I'm going to add them to our 'Writers Revise' chart right now."

WRITERS REVISE

* We reread and make plans.
* We reread, make a movie in our minds, and add words.
* We add details to our drawings.
* We add missing information.
* We add dialogue.
* We subtract things that don't build our main idea.
* We reread and think, "What parts will be confusing?"
* We show, not tell.
* Writers turn true stories into rhyming poems or exactly true poems.

This is a not a great start for a poem, but I'll lose my focus if I address that now. Resist the tangents, and resist the urge to teach everything that is in any way related.

If your children have offered no ideas for how a poem could go, it's fine for you to write a poem in the air—to say aloud one way the mouse story could have been revised as a poem.

The children are probably very immersed in the details of your instructions to rewrite the mouse story in another genre and, for now, as a non-rhyming poem. Here, I step back to name the generalizable strategy they are using, and in doing so, I remind them that the specific work with this text is just a "for instance."

"Any other ideas?"

"We thought it could be a letter."

"To whom?"

"To the principal?"

"Oh—telling her we have a mouse in our classroom! What a good idea. And might it go like this."

Dear Ms. Stock,
Last week we were reading a story and we found a mouse in our couch.

"Like that?"

The children nodded in agreement and I continued. "Okay. So that's another option and I'll add it to the chart too. Did any of you have other ideas for how we could write this?" Across the room, children put a "thumb up" sign meaning yes, they had other ideas. "I see. We could write it in other ways too. I'll add 'or . . .' to the chart to show that there are other things to do."

WRITERS REVISE

* We reread and make plans.
* We reread, make a movie in our minds, and add words.
* We add details to our drawings.
* We add missing information.
* We add dialogue.
* We subtract things that don't build our main idea.
* We reread and think, "What parts will be confusing?"
* We show, not tell.
* Writers turn true stories into rhyming poems or exactly true poems or letters or. . . .

I could solicit from children an oral version of how the letter could go, but it is also just fine (and quicker) for me to supply an example.

Once when Marie Clay visited our classrooms she said that in general, she thinks that lists rarely profit from containing more than three or four items. At some point, most lists need an "etc.," and most readers of lists should be able to imagine more items without those items being explicitly included.

Active Engagement

Ask the class to take a piece of their own writing and think about writing it in another genre.

"Writers, would you take one of your favorite stories out of your revision folders and would you think, 'Could I turn this into something else? Could I make a rhyming or an exactly true poem?' You'll need the proper paper for a poem. Or think, 'Could I make a letter? Could I make something no one else has thought of?' Stay here and reread your work by yourself, and then talk with your partner."

Link

Tell the children they can get started as soon as they've decided what to do. The children who remain on the rug may need some small-group support from you.

"When you have an idea for what you want to do today, you can get started."

Again, I hold up the paper as I speak, to make the idea of changing to a poem or letter more concrete. The different kinds of paper make a world of difference in helping children imagine the concrete requirements of this task.

In the array of possible ways to involve children actively, one option is for children to get started applying the lesson to their own work.

Children will be apt to come to you saying	In response, you might say...
"I don't know how to write a poem."	"Then you know what I'd do. I'd write it in a different way. Why not try directions (how to . . .) or a story (The little girl who. . . .)?"
"Does this look like a poem to you?"	"You know what I do when I'm trying to write something and I forget how? I read stuff like what I'm trying to write. Why don't you read this poem, and just notice a whole bunch of things the author does?"
"I can't tell if this should be a poem or a letter or what."	"You know what, almost any text can be turned into anything. For a minute, let's try the mouse story in lots of genres. What if it was a wish letter, 'Dear Mom. Please get rid of the mouse'? What if it was a speech? 'Ladies and Gentlemen, I am here today to announce that in room 209234. . . .' So yours could be anything too. Do this. Here are four sheets of paper. Give yourself eight minutes and quick, write your story as a poem on this paper, as a letter on this paper."
"I can't change mine. It doesn't go another way."	"Okay. Then start a new piece. That happens sometimes."

 These conferences in *The Conferring Handbook* may be especially helpful today:

 ▶ *"This Part Is Confusing to Me"*
 ▶ *"Can You Reenact That Part in a Way That Shows Me How You Felt?"*
 ▶ *"Study an Example to Get Ideas for Revision"*

Also, if you have *Conferring with Primary Writers*, you may want to refer to the conferences in part four:

AFTER-THE-WORKSHOP SHARE

Tell the children about one writer in the class who revised a piece into a different genre.

"Everyone, I want to share how Romi revised her story about losing her tooth into a letter! She told me I could share it with the class. Listen to the letter."

Dear Tooth Fairy,
Thank you for the five dollars so, so, so
much and please send
me a letter, Tooth Fairy.
              Love.
              Romi

"But you know what else she did? She decided she could also revise the same story as directions! Listen to her directions."

How to Loose a Tooth
1. Bite something hard
2. Try to wiggle it
3. The tooth fall out
4. Put your tooth under your pillow
5. The Tooth Fairy comes
6. The Tooth Fairy takes your tooth
7. When you wake up you get a prise
8. The end!!!

"I know that a lot of you tried revising your writing today. Would you share what you did with your partner?"[*Fig. XIII-1*]

In this share, I read Romi's pieces to the class, having asked her beforehand whether she minded. Of course, I have Romi stand beside me, and I make sure she gets the credit and the praise for sharing her work. I often get permission to do the reading myself, because I can make my teaching point more clearly and I can read more quickly. There are plenty of other occasions when I let the children read their own pieces aloud during the share.

Brianna revised her story about a sleepover to write an invitation to another one!

Dear Danielle,
Come to my house. Soon there will be a show! It will be in three weeks. There will be pictures of us! There will be flowers on walls. I'll put up decorations and you can have a sleepover. We will do the Macarena. You can try out my bed! We live on Lindmele Dr.
Love, Brianna

Fig. XIII-1 Brianna

You won't be able to resist poring over your children's work. Go to it! Along with everything else, try dividing the work into two piles. Make one pile for the youngsters whose productivity soared today, and make the other pile for those whose productivity plummeted. The piles might be revealing. Children who rose to the challenge of today's minilesson will probably be your risk takers. They may need you to help them see and make challenges for themselves more often. The children whose productivity plummeted may be likely to follow clear directions, to paint by numbers, to do as they're told to do. You'll probably want to make a point of noticing and supporting any time those children do anything out of the ordinary.

My younger sister Joan was a straight-A, straight-arrow sort of a child. When Joan was in junior high school, she lightly pushed our fully clothed gym teacher into the swimming pool. No one—least of all Joan— could figure out what had gotten into my straight-arrow sister. My parents pretended at first to be aghast but weren't able to mask for long that in fact they were delighted. Soon they were telling and retelling the story to all the relatives with a twinkle in their eyes. You may not go as far as my parents did, but do encourage children who always color inside the lines (and seem to need someone to give them coloring-book-like instructions) to be bold and to take initiative, even if this causes a bit of trouble.

LEARNING REVISION FROM AUTHORS

GETTING READY

▶ Overheads of dedication pages from several books (or the actual books)
⦿ See CD-ROM for resources

YOU'LL DELIGHT IN THE NEW ENERGY IN YOUR CLASSROOM, *but you'll no doubt also feel moments of dismay when you see a focused, sequential narrative turned into a less-well-honed letter, poem, or fiction story. Try to set aside your reservations and enjoy your children's approximations. This is the home stretch of the unit, and, depending on how you've set up your year, it may also be the home stretch before the holidays. Allow your children to glory in the new kinds of paper and in the invitation to write like fourth graders. Don't even try to micromanage their texts.*

This session will focus on one bit of generic advice that pertains to all your kids and all of their endeavors: "Whatever you are writing, find someone who has written the same sort of thing and learn from what that author has done."

THE MINILESSON

Connection

Explain to the class the value of using an experienced author to model their own writing.

"Yesterday you were writing such an amazing number of projects—songs and letters and poems and stories. Some of you decided 'I'm going to write a "something"' and then you got the paper, got your pen, sat down to write, and you thought, 'Wait a minute! I don't know how to write that thing.' This has happened to me. Today I'll show you what writers do when we want to try a new kind of writing and we are not sure how to do it."

Teaching

Teach the children that any time they set out to write a new type of writing, they can find an author who has written the same sort of thing and learn from that example. In this instance, I set out to write dedication pages and turn to authors for help.

"I'm going to tell you about what I did when I wanted to write a new kind of writing. Would you listen and see if my experience gives you ideas for what you could do now, as you try to write poems and letters and articles and directions?"

Demonstrate how you wanted to write in a particular form and found writers who'd done just that.

"When I finished my first book, the time came to write what is called the dedication. That's where you decide if you want the book to be in honor of one person, and you put a note about the person at the front of the book, on the dedication page. So I sat there and thought, 'I don't know what to write on a dedication page.'"

"You know what I did? I went over to my bookshelf and I pulled a pile of books out of the shelves and I went through them looking for books that had dedication pages. I found some people who had written dedication pages—who had written just what I was trying to write. Then I read through those and said to myself, 'Okay, so what am I learning about dedication pages?'"

Before I tell a personal story or conduct a demonstration, I set children up to listen in a particular way. Also, I describe the work we're doing as "a new kind of writing" over and over. I don't, for variety's sake, refer to it also as "new genres" or "new forms of writing." The words I use in the connection to describe what we're doing thread through the entire minilesson, giving it cohesion.

I don't simply summarize having studied the dedication pages of others. As I speak, I reenact what I actually did. I pretend I am flipping through books, quickly examining the dedications, and making a pile. I want to help students picture themselves using exemplar texts by showing how it looks to do this.

Active Engagement

Show children the examples you studied, and share your conclusions.

"Let me show you what I studied that day and see if you can learn from those dedications too." I put samples of dedications on the overhead so the whole class could see them.

> For Raymond Ryder and Arthur Charpentier, treasured fathers who nurtured their daughters with love. (From *My Father's Hands*, by Joanne Ryder)

> For Laura and Peter, who wait patiently for a Biscuit of their very own. (From *Biscuit*, by Alyssa Satin Capucilli)

After showing a couple of them, I asked children to think and talk. "Tell your partner what you are noticing about how these tend to go."

"Okay, I'm going to show you a few more. Check to see if your theory is holding."

> For my special Berry Picker and the two Little Berries. (From *Jamberry*, by Bruce Degen)

> To my mother . . . in celebration of all our summers. (From *Come On, Rain!*, by Karen Hesse)

> For Julia, who likes to practice with a string bean when she can. (From *Bread and Jam for Frances*, by Russell Hoban)

> For Mother Earth, born 4 billion years ago, and Baby Calla, born June 1, 1988, and you. (From *On the Day You Were Born*, by Debra Frasier)

"Is your theory holding? Now tell your partner three things you are learning that could help you if you wrote dedications."

Remind writers that you studied dedication pages because that's what you were writing.

"Remember, writers, that I looked at dedication pages because that's what I was writing. What if I wanted to write a recipe? Would I look at dedication pages? No!"

Link

Tell the children that they will need to find more than one example of a particular style to get an idea for what they will write. Send them off in groups according to what they're writing, with each group having a basket of exemplar texts.

"Today when you want to get some help on your writing, look for other authors who've written the same kind of thing. I have some baskets here and you'll see they are labeled *poems, directions, recipes, articles, songs,* and so forth. Point to the basket that might help *you* with *your* writing."

"Okay. Those who might want to learn from this basket of poems, take the basket, and why don't you work at the green table? Those who might learn from this basket of directions, why don't you work by the fish tank?"

This example works well for me because dedication pages are brief and easy to read and there's a lot to notice about them. You can refer to other kinds of writing. For example, you could tell about how, when a child walks a greeting card around for the teachers to sign, you feel pressured. "Oh, no, what should I say?" you think. And so you study what others have said and learn the expected format. You'd tell the kids what others said on a card and what you therefore decided to say. Even the signs on our classroom doors can pose a challenge—and we can learn from studying what others have done on their doors.

TIME TO CONFER

Remember that you can solicit authors of published texts to be co-teachers, showing children what's possible. Carry a short stack of mentor texts with you and get used to saying to children, "You seem to be writing a bit like (so and so). Why don't I leave this with you? I just know that if you study what this author has done, it'll give you some ideas for your writing." The children may not notice the most essential features, but the fact that they look at the work of another author thinking, "What has this author done that I could try in my writing?" is no small feat! See the conferences cited at right.

 This conference in *The Conferring Handbook* may be especially helpful today:

▶ *"Study an Example to Get Ideas for Revision"*

Also, if you have *Conferring with Primary Writers*, you may want to refer to the following conference:

▶ "Let's Look at Your Lead and Your Ending"

Help kids realize that when they first do something, they should expect to be surprised and to learn.

"Would you think about the first time you ever lost a tooth? Were you surprised about anything? Did you learn something the first time you ever lost a tooth? Tell your partner one thing you learned the first time you lost a tooth." I watched and listened. Then I reconvened the class.

"I'm excited because this is a class of smart learners. You all learned something the first time you lost a tooth. Smart learners try to learn whenever we do something for the first time. So I'm hoping that when you revised your stories into a different kind of writing, something surprised you. I'm hoping that in the end you have a new piece of writing *and* a new lesson that you learned from trying this work."

"Right now, let's sit and think. Think of a lesson you learned by taking your story and revising it to make a different kind of writing. Thumbs up if you've thought of your lesson."

"For the rest of your lives, remember that the first time you do anything, you can expect to learn a lot. And remember, too, that smart writers don't only *do* things—we also *learn* things."

If you have time, ask children to talk about the lessons they learned with a partner and perhaps elicit a few of these lessons. But don't feel obliged to do this.

If Children Need More Time

If you decide to give your children some extra time, which they will certainly be able to use, you can try the following:

- Use your own work to show how one idea (for example, your grandmother's eighty-fifth birthday party) can be turned into a bunch of different genres. Don't just talk about it, have written examples to read to the children. For example, you may have written a Small Moment piece on the birthday party and you may now produce a poem, a newspaper article, an invitation, a birthday card, a list of things to get for the party, a how-to book about baking a birthday cake, a weather report, directions to the park where the party was held, and so on. You'll find different aspects of the experience are brought out in the different genres.
- Highlight the way one child made reading-writing connections. Show the exemplar text the child read (just the particular page), and then show a section of the child's writing in which she emulated the author.
- Have a bit of shared writing the class has already written. This might be a text as simple as the sign on your classroom door or the label in your block corner. Then show a similar text written by other authors and ask the class to join you in studying the exemplar to get ideas for how to improve the original bit of shared writing. Elicit a few things they've noticed and redo the original text with the help of this new input.

PREPARING TO CELEBRATE

GETTING READY

▶ "Writers Revise" chart
▶ Sticky note tags for each child
▶ Bulletin board, ready to display children's work
▶ Time and wherewithal to duplicate pages children select
▶ Marker pens and construction paper
▶ Thumbtacks or stapler for putting writing on the bulletin board
● See CD-ROM for resources

SOMETIMES UNITS WIND DOWN IN THEIR FINAL DAYS, *but it's not likely this one will! Nevertheless, you and your children will have devoted a good amount of time to studying revision, and it's time for their work to culminate in a celebration. Your children will have revised lots of writing; each of the revised pieces deserves to be published and reach readers. Inventory your resources and decide how many publications you can support.*

It's great if you can get a few parents to volunteer for a day or two so that each child can bring a published book home as a holiday gift. You'll want to print a second and perhaps a third copy of that book for the class and maybe the school library. Ideally, over the upcoming holidays, you or someone else can word-process a second book by each child, again printing out several copies, so that in the end, each of your children can have two books in their parents' archives and two on the shelves of their classroom and in the school library.

For now, you'll also want children to celebrate by telling others the story of their revision work. It's important to take some time to celebrate not only the new learning that took place in this unit, but also the product. Today, you turn over the session to the students, asking them to teach others what they've done and learned in this unit on revision. Use minilesson time for your children to talk about their learning. It is an opportunity for you and the children to see how they've grown as writers. The unit has focused on revision, so you'll want your author celebration to showcase revision.

In this session, you will prepare the children to teach others about revision.

The Minilesson

Connection

Tell the children about the growth you've seen across the unit, and ask if they are willing to teach others what they've learned.

"Writers, do you remember the first day of this unit, when I asked you if you were really proud of your writing—and then I told you that when writers really care about their writing, we revise it?"

"You've all given a lot of loving care to your writing. Your writing has grown strong and detailed and lovely and long because you've taken such care of it, because you've revised it so well. Now it's time to celebrate the work you've done. As part of our celebration, I was thinking that maybe you'd be willing to teach other people what you've learned about revision. Would you be willing to do that?"

The children chorused, "Yes!"

Teaching and Active Engagement

Suggest that the class turn their "Writers Revise" chart into a bulletin board, with each bullet being a separate section belonging to a small group of writers. Ask the children to search their work for examples of each revision strategy.

"I was thinking that maybe we could take our 'Writers Revise' chart and make a huge bulletin board in the hall. So one part of the bulletin board could say, 'We add details to our drawings,' and then you could display places in your books where you *really did that*. Another part of the bulletin board could be, 'We add dialogue,' and if any of you did that, we could copy those pages and hang them up there—to show other kids and visitors to the school, too."

I know this unit is coming to a close and so it makes sense to harken back to the beginning of the unit, reflecting on the journey.

I try to help children understand that revision is a way to honor and care for one's writing. Too often, youngsters grow up thinking of revision as a form of punishment.

This minilesson doesn't fit our usual template.

Link

Send a small group of writers to find examples of "we add dialogue," and so on.

"Let's have three writers be in charge of each section of the bulletin board, so Heather, George, and Ezra, will you look through your revision folders and see if you can find a page that shows a time you added dialogue? If you find a few pages, put a sticky note tag on the best and I'll copy them for the bulletin board. And you also need to make a big sign that says 'Writers Add Dialogue.' Patrick, Lisa, and Romi, would you look for a few examples of showing, not telling, and make a sign that says 'Writers Show, Not Tell'? Eric, Larry, and Emma, will you look for places you revised your leads and then you can make the sign that says 'Writers Revise Their Leads. . . .'"

"In your group, look first through your own writing and then, if you need more examples, look through other kids' writing. Look for places where you did whatever your section describes. Use sticky note tags to mark all the examples you find, and then reread them together and choose two or three particularly good examples, written by different kids, for me to copy on the copy machine. Okay?"

You will probably want to select the members of each work group so that each group contains writers whose revisions fit their assigned category. You may or may not want each group to coauthor a blurb full of hints and ideas for using this revision strategy.

The bulletin board can later become a book called "Writers Revise," with each bullet from the chart, each subsection from the bulletin board, becoming a new chapter.

TIME TO CONFER

Your conferring today will need to be very goal-directed. Bring some parents in and see if they, too, can help you to organize your revision museum. Your children will learn a lot from being asked to review their work and to select examples of different kinds of revision that they've done. You, meanwhile, can record what they and you see on your conferring checklist for this unit of study.

These conferences in *The Conferring Handbook* may be especially helpful today:

▶ *"This Part Is Confusing to Me"*

▶ *"Can You Reenact That Part in a Way That Shows Me How You Felt?"*

▶ *"Study an Example to Get Ideas for Revision"*

Also, if you have *Conferring with Primary Writers*, you may want to refer to the conferences in part four.

Setting Up a Revision Museum: An Author's Celebration

Getting Ready

- Send out invitations
- Ask each child to choose pieces to share in the revision museum
- Help children practice teaching others the process they used to revise their pieces
- Assign each child a spot—a "booth"—in which to display his or her work
- Set up a bell or signal to let people know it is time to visit another child
- Provide treats, juice, and cups for the toast
- See CD-ROM for resources

YOUNG CHILDREN KEEP US IN TOUCH *with the need for celebration. Because we are teachers, there's not much chance that Valentine's Day or Halloween will slip by us unnoticed. How lucky we are to be in a profession that reminds us that life is richer when it is punctuated by a sense of occasion!*

The writing workshop, too, becomes richer when it is punctuated by a sense of occasion. At the start of the year, children will be thrilled simply to read their writing aloud, to toast themselves as authors, and to eat a celebratory cookie. The challenge is to be sure that as the months go by, each Author's Celebration feels momentous to our youngsters.

One way to keep the energy high is to vary our celebrations. In Pat's classroom, we decided to invite parents, administrators, and older students, and to turn the school library into a revision museum. Each child was given his or her own "booth," and the child found a way to display work in progress that showed what he or she had done. To draw observers' attention to places where the children had made especially key revisions, these young authors put little "Ask Me" sticky note tags at particular places throughout their texts.

The day before our museum opened the children gave out invitations, chose pieces that showed their revisions, and practiced explaining how they revised their work during a dry run with writing partners (and, for some children, with Pat and me). This preparation added to their excitement.

In this celebration, students will create a revision museum, explain to visiting guests what they learned about revision, and receive written responses about their stories from their guests.

THE CELEBRATION

Before the visitors enter the "museum," explain the procedures.

Pat and I welcomed the visitors and gave each visitor a list of the children they were to visit (in order). The last child on each visitor's list was that visitor's own child. We explained that we'd sound a bell every so often to let people know they only had two more minutes and would then need to move to the next child. We asked each visitor to fill in each child's response sheet, writing one very specific thing they admired that the child had done.

Have the children stand by their stations, waiting for the visitors to arrive.

Taylor said, "I hope I remember what to say."

George responded, "If you forget, look at our chart."

Lisa joined in, "I know what to say. I practiced."

Have the children share their revisions with the visitors.

The parents entered and went to each child's station. The children explained how they revised their pieces. Samantha said, "I used 'show, not tell' to show I was angry. You see it says right here, 'I stamped my foot!'" George showed how he used a flap to add more details to his story. Romi showed how she changed her true story into a "How to Lose a Tooth" book and then into a letter to the tooth fairy. At the signal, visitors moved to another child. At every station, visitors busily recorded responses to the child's work.

Gather to toast all that the children have accomplished.

After about forty minutes, Pat closed our museum. "Writers and visitors, please join me for a toast to our wonderful writers!" The children and visitors all got cups of juice and gathered to raise a toast.

"I hoped you enjoyed coming to our revision museum and that you learned how we revised our writing to make it better. Writers, you have worked so hard! You learned how to go back and reread, to add on, and to take out. You learned to add dialogue and details and to show, not tell. You have built wonderful writing, and I am so proud of all of you! Let's toast our amazing writers."